Customs of Cambodia

Zhou Daguan

Customs of Cambodia

Zhou Daguan

Based on the Original Chinese Manuscript
by author Zhou Daguan of Yongjia, Yuan Dynasty.
Published by Wu Guan of Xin'an, Ming Dynasty

Translated and Annotated by
Solang and Beling Uk

Edited by
Kent Davis

DatAsia Press

2016

About the cover:

When Zhou Daguan arrived in Cambodia in 1296 AD, the state shrine of the Bayon was the focal point of the walled city of Angkor Thom. As seen in the author's photo, its four faces look to the four cardinal directions, symbolizing the Khmer king's power extending into the universe. Artist Rebecca Klein created a vibrant cover from Khmer elements, capturing the excitement of Zhou's eye-witness account in this new translation.

About the translators:

Solang Uk is a native of Touk Meas, Cambodia. In the 1950s, Madeleine Giteau—renowned French historian on Khmer culture and member of the Ecole Française d'Extrême-Orient—was his history teacher for two years when he attended Lycée Sisowath in Phnom-Penh. Since completing his Ph. D. in biology at the University of Georgia, USA, Solang worked as a senior research scientist at Cranfield Institute of Technology, England, then at Ciba-Geigy Ltd. and Novartis AG, Switzerland. Solang authored and co-authored 50 scientific papers that were published in 12 scientific journals and 17 books and monographs.

Beling Uk, his wife, is a native of Hunan, China. She graduated in biology from The National Taiwan University and North Carolina State University. She worked as a microbiologist in the Carlsberg Group in Switzerland.
Solang and Beling are now retired and living in Switzerland where they enjoy working on cultural research projects like this translation

DatASIA Press — www.DatASIA.us

© Copyright 2016. DatASIA, Inc., Holmes Beach, FL 34218

ISBN 978-1-934431-18-4

Library of Congress Control Number: 2015951579

Printed simultaneously in the United States of America and Great Britain.

In memory of Amir D. Aczel,
and his successful quest of
"Finding Zero"
in the Kingdom of Cambodia.

November 6, 1950 – November 26, 2015

TABLE OF CONTENTS

CUSTOMS OF CAMBODIA - ZHOU DAGUAN

APPENDICES

ACKNOWLEDGEMENTS

We would like to thank Tan Seng Hoc for introducing Solang to Mr. Ly Thiam Kheng (Ly Thiam Teng's brother) who in turn, helped Solang to meet Mrs. Ly Thiam Teng and her son (Ly Suratha). Ly Thiam Kheng provided us with a copy of his brother's original Khmer translation of Zhou Daguan's Record. Mrs. Ly Thiam Teng kindly allowed us to make use of the content of her late husband's book in whatever way we wish.

Thanks are also due to Mrs. Wesley Hsu who provided us with a copy of **Zhou Daguan's** Record (**Zhenla feng tu ji**) in Chinese by **Jin Ronghua** and to Mrs. Tai-Yen Pao for the copy of another Chinese re-publication of **Zhenla feng tu ji** by **Xia Nai**. Tek Angri, Tek Nirano, and Yam Chhann provided maps, photos, and valuable information on place names and Khmer traditions. We thank most sincerely Sun Sea Pao, Tai-Yen Pao, Sue Chiu for their most valuable comments.

Special thanks are due to Mr. Boun Suy Tan, Deputy Director General of Apsara Authority, Cambodia, Prof. Charles Higham and Prof. Claude Jacques for their encouraging comments on this publication.

We thank Ms. Veronica Walker Vadillo for her valuable photo of a partially completed dugout boat, and Asger M. Mollerup for his Dharmasala Route map from Angkor to Phimai. The guidance of editor Kent Davis in preparing this new edition is gratefully appreciated.

Finally, heartfelt thanks to Dr. Amir Aczel's wife, Mrs. Debra Gross Aczel, and his daughter, Ms. Miriam Rose Aczel, for sharing their photos of Amir's journey of discovery and for keeping his voice alive to continue his educational mission.

Amir Dan Aczel with stele K-127 in Cambodia.

FOREWORD

It is a great pleasure to open this important translation of Zhou Daguan by Solang and Beling Uk. Through an unexpected series of events my connection to, and admiration for, the Khmer people is very personal.

After authoring 20 academic books I decided to satisfy a lifetime obsession to discover the mathematical origins of numbers. My quest was intensified by what was, to me, the most intriguing question: Who invented the abstract concept of "zero"? My search for this knowledge became a global odyssey, culminating in the jungles of ancient Cambodia.

From clues in Indian philosophy, and the religions of Hinduism, Jainism and Buddhism, I theorized that the number system we know today originated in the East. One iconic representation that inspired me was that of the Hindu god Vishnu. In it, Vishnu reclines in slumber upon the sea serpent, Ananta, in the infinite cosmic ocean until his consort, Lakshmi, awakens him. It is then that Brahma, the creator of the worlds, manifests from a lotus flower on Vishnu's stomach. From nothingness comes everything. This was the promise of my quest for "zero."

My archival research led me to the work of imminent Southeast Asian archaeologist, historian and Khmer epigraphist Georges Cœdès, former Director of L'Ecole Française d'Extrême Orient. In 1931, Cœdès published a paper about a stone stele discovered in Sambaur district in the northeastern province of Kratié, possibly a Pre-Angkorian capital (debatable among historians) of Zhenla (or Chenla) known originaly as Sambhupura. What caught my attention was that the inscription included the numeral "605" indicating the Saka year corresponding to AD 683. Coedès conducted detailed research and contended that this is the first numeral zero, predating Indian or Arabic numerals.

More than 70 years ago, the stele—named K-127 by Coedès—was displayed in the National Museum in Phnom Penh. Tragically, that peaceful country descended into war and genocide at the hands of the communist Khmer Rouge government in 1975. These fanatics murdered more than a million people, as they destroyed the foundation of Khmer society along with thousands of irreplaceable historical records and archaeological artifacts. Did K-127 also fall victim to this senseless violence? I decided to travel to Cambodia to find out.

ព្រះនរាយណ៍ផ្ទុំ
ប្រាសាទមេបុណ្យខាងលិចអង្គរ ខេត្តសៀមរាប
សម័យអង្គរ រចនាបថបាគង ស.វ. ទី១១ - សំរឹទ្ធ

Fig. 00-00. Reclining Vishnu found in Prasat West Mebon (fig. 01-12) that Zhou Daguan called bronze reclining Buddha in East Baray (Photo S. Uk, 2016 with permission from the National Museum in Phnom Penh).

As recounted in my 2015 book "Finding Zero" I prepared to set out to Southeast Asia, knowing I would follow the footsteps of an unusual fellow traveller. In the 13th century, Zhou Daguan, a member of Chinese diplomatic mission, travelled to Cambodia which was then home to the fabulous Khmer Empire. Zhou's "Record on Cambodia" remains unique today because it is the oldest and most detailed account of ancient Cambodia and its legendary capital city of Angkor, known then as Yaśodharapura.

From Cambodia's earliest days it adopted ideologies from both the Hindu and Buddhist religions from India. From Hinduism, Khmer kings adapted their local concepts of architecture and city planning to represent the cosmic world. They built enormous "temple mountains" as symbols of Mount Meru—the center of the universe—surrounded by cosmic oceans represented by huge artificial lakes called Baray.

Zhou described the temple city in detail. Although a few of his distance and size measurements were incorrect, his reports of the society and its structures resonate with accuracy. At the centre of one large Baray he described a stone tower with a chamber at its centre. Within the chamber he noted a large bronze statue with water flowing from its navel. He described it as a reclining Buddha—the most familiar religious statue to the Chinese at the time—but in fact it represented Vishnu, reflecting the idea that Brahma sprang out of Vishnu's navel. Today, part of that statue rests in the National Museum of Cambodia. But what of K-127?

As I describe in "Finding Zero," my circuitous Cambodian adventure ultimately united me with the long lost inscription proving the first use of zero by the Khmer people (see my original photo on p. 58 of this book). I also saw the actual Khmer image of Vishnu, described by Zhou centuries ago, embodying my vision of everything springing from nothing. So much good can come from curiosity, old manuscripts and diligent research which brings us back to this present volume.

Though Zhou Daguan's journal was previously translated to French and then to English, this edition offers readers the first direct translation from ancient Chinese by authors born in Cambodia and China. This is why it is such a pleasure to endorse this new translation by Solang and Beling Uk.

Seeing many errors in the interpretations and annotations of previous translators, Solang (a native Cambodian) and Beling (a native Chinese) were inspired to translate one of Zhou's original Chinese texts directly to English. As trained biologists and natives of the cultures described, they read the original account from a perspective far deeper than that of prior archaeologists, linguists and historians.

This resulting work refines nuances of translation, rectifies misinterpretations and clarifies dubious passages while adding photographs, maps and drawings to bring the plants, temples, people and animals of Zhou's original record to life. I invite you to enjoy their work, which for generations to come will serve as a valuable tool for scholars of Cambodia as well as an entertaining guide for all visitors to the renowned ancient city of Angkor.

Amir D. Aczel

Professor of Mathematics
University of Massachusetts, Boston

FOREWORD ADDENDUM

Amir Aczel died at age 65 on November 26, 2015 in Nimes, France. While he cared deeply about a wide range of subjects from mathematics to physics to the history of science, he was particularly passionate about calling the world's attention to the remarkable role Angkor civilization played in the history of mathematics.

At the time of his death, Amir was working with the Cambodian government and the Ministry of Culture to install in the Cambodian National Museum the K127 stele containing the oldest zero ever discovered. He dreamed of Cambodians and international visitors alike learning of the importance of this discovery. He further hoped to establish a conference to bring together mathematicians, historians and scholars from all over the world to celebrate this monumental contribution of the Cambodian people. He envisioned scholarly sessions in which papers would be presented on the importance of zero to mathematics. He also hoped to use this event as a way to draw attention to the greater glories of Cambodian culture.

Although he is no longer with us, we have established the Amir D. Aczel Foundation for Research and Education in Science and Mathematics to work toward fulfilling these goals.

Debra Gross Aczel
Miriam Rose Aczel

Preface to the 2nd Edition

Nothing new is known about **Zhou Daguan's** Record on The Land and Customs of Cambodia since the meticulous translation and annotations by Paul Pelliot in 1902 and 1951 (published posthumously). Prof. **Jin Ronghua** in Taiwan (1976) and **Xia Nai** (2000) in the PRC (People's Republic of China), independently made detailed study in Chinese so that the original **Zhou Daguan's** text can be understood by ordinary readers since it was written in ancient classical Chinese where one ordinary long sentence is condensed into just a few Chinese characters. Both Chinese authors also refer to a lot of Pelliot's annotations.

The purpose of this second edition is to include some pictures that would support the identification of the controversial places such as **Fu Cun** （佛村）(the Buddha Village), or the sculptures on the Bayon bas-reliefs representing the sugar palm tree, or **Zhou Daguan's ta** （塔）that the King always takes with him in his procession out of the palace which we think is the sacrificial fire (Kandvar Homa). Sculptures on the walls of Bayon temple illustrate the many aspects of the daily life in the Angkor period. Yet **Zhou Daguan**'s record sometimes contradicts those illustrations, e.g. the armements of soldiers, and makes one wonders whether he had free access to the temples.

Solang & Beling Uk
Switzerland, March 2016

1st Edition Preface

Cambodia was a dominant power that ruled most of mainland southeast Asia for 500 years from the 9th to the 14th centuries from its capital, known today as Angkor. After the fall of the empire, Angkor was abandoned and left to the invading forest until it was rediscovered and made known to the West by the French explorer, Henri Mouhot in the 1860s. However, Mouhot was not the first Westerner to have discovered Angkor. Two Portuguese travellers, the trader Diogo do Coto and the monk Antonio da Magdalena, wrote accounts of their visits to Angkor in 1550 and 1586 respectively.

Little was known of the social structure and organization of the empire apart from what appeared in stone inscriptions and sculptures on walls of the monuments. Documents written on perishable materials (leather and palm leaves) had disappeared long ago due to the destructive power of the tropical climate. In 1296, **Zhou Daguan**, a member of the Chinese diplomatic mission of the Mongol Emperor Temür Khan, spent almost one year in Angkor. After returning to China, he wrote detailed accounts of Cambodia, its land and the customs of its people. This is the only surviving written record that enables us to have a glimpse into life in Cambodia at the end of the 13th century AD. In China, **Zhou Daguan**'s Record has been republished many times through the centuries - some parts have possibly been lost, others altered or wrongly reproduced.

In 1819, a French physician and sinologist, Jean-Pierre Abel-Ramusat published the first French translation of **Zhou Daguan**'s Record on Cambodia. Paul Pelliot, also a French sinologist and explorer, published his own French translation of **Zhou**'s Record in 1902. A newer edition, which includes Pelliot's revised translation with more detailed annotations was published posthumously in 1951. Subsequently, there have been English and German translations of Pelliot's work. Aschmoneit (2006) published a German translation of Pelliot's text with modifications and adaptations from two new Chinese editions, one by **Jin Ronghua** (1976) and the other by **Xia Nai** (1981). In 2007 Peter Harris published an English translation from Chinese texts. All the translations to date into French, German and English have been done by Westerners with different concepts and understanding of the Chinese and Khmer (Cambodian) culture. Often they are not aware of the subtle nuances of meaning of words and customs.

As a Khmer (Solang) and a Chinese (Beling), we are far from satisfied with all existing published translations, however meticulous they appear to be. Pelliot is the undeniable authority on **Zhou Daguan**'s Record on Cambodia. His detailed work on the translation rightly earned him praise and respect from all of us. However, some of his interpretations were, and remain, off course to this day. For example, Pelliot who originally thought that **Zhou**'s Buddha Village was Bâribaur near Kampong Chhnang, i.e., near the river Tonle Sap, later agreed with Coedès (1989) that the Buddha village is the town of Pôsat (French spelling: Pursat). This is a false identification and remains to this day. It has been quoted and re-quoted in many publications.

Even the 20th century Chinese scholar, **Xia Nai**, included an incorrect map in his annotated re-edition of **Zhou**'s Record. In reality, the town of Pôsat has nothing to do with being a Buddha town. The Khmer spelling of Pôsat (ពោធិសាត់) is completely different from that for Bodhisattva (ពោធិសត្វ) or Buddha. Unless one knows the details of the Khmer alphabet, the local culture, literature and local tales, one cannot derive a correct conclusion from a superficial reading - in this case the homophone 'sat'.

The late George Coedès was an authority on the Khmer epigrapy and the Khmer language, yet he overlooked the Khmer spelling of Pôsat. Far from being a town that implies Buddha, the legend of Pôsat town is as follows: once upon a time, there was a Bodhi tree seedling drifting (Khmer: "rô sat") strangely upstream against the river current. It came to rest on the river bank beside the village. People picked it up and planted it near to where it had been lodged, and called the village "Pô rô sat" meaning 'the drifting Bodhi tree'. As time went by, the name evolved and lost the word "rô" and became simply "Pô sat" (French: Pursat) (Dictionnaire Cambodgien, 1967). Again, we would like to emphasize that the Khmer spelling for Pôsat town is very different from the spelling for Buddha or Bodhisattva. Thus, the Latin alphabet transliteration of the town's name should be "Pôsat" and not "Pôthisat" as stipulated by Coedès. Furthermore, the town of Pôsat is more than 25km inland, away from Tonle Sap Lake where **Zhou** was sailing towards Angkor. He could not possibly have passed by Pôsat. It is regrettable that this wrong assumption on the 'Buddha village' has been repeated by many scholars for more than a century even to this day (e.g. **Xia Nai** 2000).

In modern day Cambodia, there is a village called Kampong Preah (= Buddha dock or port) at the entrance of Tonle Sap Lake in the sub-district of Chhnok Trou, province of Kampong Chhnang. As it is on the river bank along the waterway leading to Angkor, Kampong Preah (Buddha port) is the most likely village **Zhou** was referring to.

Another point that is obvious to a Chinese and a Khmer but not to people from other cultures, is the transliteration of Khmer words into Chinese. Since the written Chinese uses monosyllabic characters, it cannot faithfully transliterate the consonant clusters that are common in the alphabetical Khmer – a single Khmer cluster consonant is written as two Chinese characters then read and pronounced as two syllables. There are many 'monosyllabic' Khmer words with cluster consonants that end up as two Chinese characters throughout **Zhou Daguan's** text. Transliteration problems, however difficult, can still yield reasonable understanding through inference. On the other hand, wrong translation and/or wrong interpretation of place, plant and animal names, impart on generations of readers and researchers distorted information. There have been many such errors in the literature on **Zhou**'s Record and we will attempt to correct them by making relevant annotations on some of these errors.

My (Solang's) interest in Angkor dates back to my childhood in the 1940s. When I was four years old (1943), in one of his bedtime stories, my father told me that Angkor Wat was built overnight by Preah Visnukar (a celestial architect/engineer) for his earthly son, King Preah Ket Mealea. Later in school, I realized that my father's bedtime story was just a legend[1]. The early history of the Khmer (Cambodian) people itself is mingled in legends, most of them inspired by Hindu mythology, and are subsequently quoted in many history books. Respectable scholars (Khmers and others) would sometimes credulously take legends as historical facts. Who knows where legend ends and history begins?

History lessons in school taught me that Angkor Wat was built by King Suryavarman II and there was nothing magical or celestial about the construction of the monument that took more than twenty years to complete. My history teacher of the 'classes de 5eme and 4eme moderne' (2nd and 3rd year of secondary school), Ms. Madeleine Giteau[2] was a charming young French lady, but a tough disciplinarian who made me learn history in detail. Students were taught that Khmer history during the Angkor period was based mainly on the records of a Chinese visitor, **Zhou Daguan**, translated into French by Paul Pelliot.

In 1960, I had the privilege to visit Angkor and the fact that the big American school bus I was in could go through the comparatively small gate of Angkor Thom remains in my memory to this day. The bus sped towards the south gate of Angkor Thom. Anxiety arose in me and some of my travelling companions because the gate looked too low and narrow. We all said; "Will the bus go through? Maybe not". While we were anxiously looking fore and aft, port and starboard, a dark shadow seemed to pass overhead and then in a flash we were at the other side of the gate, inside the old Great City (Angkor Thom = big city).

In 1963 I left Cambodia to continue my studies in the USA. I forgot then about Angkor and its history. Seven years went by and to my disbelief the Vietnam War suddenly spilled over full scale into Cambodia, practically overnight, in a way similar to that of the large bus entering the gate of Angkor Thom in a flash in 1960. I was then forced to be on self-imposed exile. I finished my university studies in the USA with a Ph.D. in Biology and obtained a research position with a Swiss multinational company based in England.

One day in 1994 while passing through Bangkok airport on one of my business trips, I saw and bought an English translation of Pelliot's French version of **Zhou Daguan**'s Record on the Customs of Cambodia, by J. Gilman d'Arcy Paul (3rd edition, 1993). This brought back memories of my youth and renewed my interest on Angkor. Alas, I was still unable to visit Cambodia as the civil war raged on.

Thirty-three years were to pass before I could briefly set foot in my beloved Cambodia again. I returned three years later and every year afterwards for the next five years.

In 2004, I saw on a bookstall a Khmer version of **Zhou**'s Record on Cambodia (probably a pirated print of the 1973 edition). This had been translated from an old Chinese document by a reputed Cambodian writer, Ly Thiam Teng. I tried to trace Mr. Ly Thiam Teng to find out whether or not he had survived the war and the Khmer Rouges. Eventually, I met his younger brother (Ly Thiam Kheng) who was living in Paris. He gave me the address of Mrs. Ly Thiam Teng and her son who lived in Phnom-

Penh, Cambodia, and a copy of the 1973 edition of Ly Thiam Teng's book. I realized then that the Khmer book I had found in Phnom-Penh was indeed a pirated publication since the picture representing a Khmer man (of the Angkor period) on the front cover had been erroneously redrawn. The genuine 1973 edition had a reproduction of the original Chinese gravure (Fig. 06-01) which showed the Khmer man wearing the ubiquitous Khmer shawl (krâmā) on his head. In the pirated copy, the man is bare-headed.

I met Mrs. Ly Thiam Teng and her son in Phnom-Penh in 2005. Unfortunately, Mr. Ly Thiam Teng did not survive the brutal Khmer Rouge regime that ruled Cambodia between 1975 and 1979. The Chinese document and the original Khmer translation work, as well as the Ly's family house, were lost in the turmoil. Mrs. Ly is now living in a small apartment in a Phnom-Penh suburb.

In 1962, Mr. Ly Thiam Teng was sent by the Cambodian government on a cultural exchange visit to Beijing, leading a delegation of Khmer Writers. He took this opportunity to try to find documents on Zhou Daguan's Record on Cambodia. After persistent requests to the Chinese Minister of Culture, he was finally allowed to consult rare Chinese books at the Beijing National Library and obtained permission to microfilm Wu Guan's edition of Zhou Daguan's Record. Upon his return to Cambodia, he had two copies of prints made from the microfilm and then he translated the document into Khmer and published the first edition in 1971.

I now have the French translation by P. Pelliot (1951 edition reprinted in 1997), the English translation by J. Gilman d'Arcy Paul (1993), the revised (updated) English version by M. Smithies (2001) and the Khmer version by Ly Thiam Teng. Reading all these translations, I developed a feeling of dissatisfaction and a desire to find at least one Chinese text. Searching through the Internet, I found among the few republications of **Zhou Daguan**'s Record, one by **Jin Ronghua** (**Taipei** 1976) and another by **Xia Nai** (**Beijing** 2000). I managed to obtain a copy of each of these publications. In the meantime in Cambodia, I came across a small booklet reproducing the original Chinese block prints of **Wu Guan**'s edition. I wonder whether this is a reproduction from Ly Thiam Teng's microfilm prints which had been lost (Appendix A).

Having seen the various interpretation errors and the annotations that sometimes create more confusion than clarification in all the published translations to date, we, as a Khmer and a Chinese, felt compelled to take up the challenge to translate **Zhou Daguan**'s Record on Cambodia. Our aim is to contribute to the further understanding of **Zhou**'s text by refining translation nuances, rectifying interpretation errors, and clarifying doubtful passages (e.g. the Buddha village, palm trees, leprosy, the **tubu** fish, etc.) so that the English readership can have a better source of information rather than continue to refer to the same mistakes in publication after publication. We are using **Wu Guan**'s edition as the basis for the translation instead of the more popular **Shuo fu** edition (known from 1646-47) used by other translators, and it may have fewer modifications by subsequent Chinese editors. In doing our translation, we have tried to maintain the balance between keeping faithfully to the spirit of **Zhou**'s text and making the English as clear and grammatically correct as possible. The Chinese words or sounds transliterated from Khmer by **Zhou Daguan** are put into **pinyin** form in bold letters. **Zhou** wrote his Record in an old classic style with concise, short words and expressions that imply long sentences and meaning. To help interpret **Zhou**'s text, we refer to both the scholarly publications by **Jin Ronghua** (1976) and by **Xia Nai** (2000).

Does our new translation serve any useful purpose? It certainly does. As native Khmer and Chinese, we can make more useful contributions, by correcting inaccuracies and errors of interpretation that have been published and further quoted in many publications to date.

Both of us are biologists, educated first in our native countries then in the USA. Besides our inherited customs and perceptions of Cambodia and China, we also know the geography of the two countries and their flora and fauna sufficiently well to determine with reasonable certainty the places and plant and animal species **Zhou Daguan** recorded. We have often found errors in existing published work, be it of western translators or of 20th century Chinese scholars who re-published **Zhou**'s report. In short, our book can help in rectifying misguided information and deciphering certain passages that have been hitherto unclear or unidentified so that readers can visualize fully what **Zhou Daguan** had seen in Cambodia in the 13th century.

Being neither archaeologists nor historians, we adopt Occam's razor approach, i.e. using the simplest explanations available without delving into ancient sources in China or India that sometimes create more confusion than clarification. After all **Zhou** wrote about things Cambodian, but with his Chinese perception as reference. Our aim is to present a simple and easy appreciation of the information recorded by **Zhou Daguan** to the readers, particularly when they visit Angkor.

Zhou Daguan presented his Record in the form of topics each with a clear heading. Many translated texts on social customs and ranks, places, plants, animals, etc., require extensive explanatory remarks. These can cause inconvenience with reading interruptions and distractions. To help maintain the flow of reading, we have numbered each topic as a chapter and put relevant notes immediately after each one. Since Cambodians call themselves Khmer (the people and the language), we use the words Cambodian and Khmer interchangeably throughout the book.

We sincerely appreciate the help and support of many people in providing essential documents and photos, in reading and making constructive comments that finally resulted in the shape of the present book. However, we (the translators) take full responsibility for errors and inaccuracies that may occur despite our careful research and interpretation.

Solang & Beling Uk
Switzerland, June 2010

---

(1) This legend is known throughout Cambodia with slight local variations (Porée and Maspéro 1938 and Marchal 1955).

(2) Madeleine Giteau (1918 – 2005) was a French historian and member of the Ecole Française d'Extrême-Orient, who devoted a great part of her life to research on the art and archaeology of Cambodia. In the 1950s she taught history at Lycée Sisowath and Lycée Descartes in Phnom-Penh while holding the directorship of the National Museum.

CUSTOMS OF CAMBODIA

ZHOU DAGUAN

INTRODUCTION

The country **Zhenla**[1] is also called **Zhanla**. The natives call their own country **Ganbozhi**[2]. The present holy dynasty, following the Tibetan Buddhist Holy Book[3], calls this country **Ganpuzhi** which sounds like **Ganbozhi**. We embarked at **Wenzhou** and sailed south by southwest past the ports in **Fujian** and **Guangdong** [Provinces] and overseas ports[4], then crossed the Seven-Islands Sea[5] passed **Jiaozhi** Sea[6] and arrived in Champa[7]. Then we sailed downwind for half a month before arriving at **Zhenpu**[8] which is the border of this country. From **Zhenpu**, we sailed 1/6 west of southwest direction, traversed the **Kunlun** Sea[9] and arrived at the estuaries[10]. There were more than ten waterways. Only the fourth was navigable because most were so shallow and sandy, a large ship could not pass through. Everywhere we looked was covered with lianas, old trees, yellow sand and white reeds[11]. At first glance, we could not recognize our way easily. So the sailers found it difficult to locate the entry passage. From this entry estuary, we travelled northward upstream along the river for about half a month to reach a place called **Zhanan**[12] which is the name of a province of this country. From **Zhanan**, we changed to a smaller boat, travelled downstream for more than ten days passing through the Half-Way Village[13], the Buddha Village[14] and across the Fresh-Water Sea[15] to reach **Ganbang**[16]. From here to the city is fifty **li**[17] [about 25km].

According to the 'Various Records on Foreign Countries'[18], this country measures 7,000 **li**, bordering Champa to the North which takes half a month to reach [by road]. To the Southwest is Siam which is also half a month away [from Angkor]. Ten days' journey southward one could reach **Panyu**[19]. The frontier to the East[20] is the ocean.

Our country has had continuous commercial relations with this country since olden times. Our Holy Dynasty received the honorary mandate from heaven to spread our rule to the Four Seas[21]. Generalissimo **Suo Dou**[22] set up our administrative province in Champa. He had sent two high officials to **Zhenla**, one **wanhu**[23] bearing the tiger plate, and one **qianhu**[24] bearing the gold plate. These two were arrested and did not return.

In the 6th month of the first year of the **Yuanzhen** epoch, year **yiwei**[25], the Holy Son of The Heaven[26] sent out an envoy to remind [**Zhenla**] of its obligations. I was sent along. In the 2nd lunar month of the following year, year **bingshen**, we left **Mingzhou**[27]. On the 20th day [of the 2nd lunar month], we embarked at **Wenzhou**[28] and sailed to the open sea. On the 15th of the 3rd lunar month we arrived in Champa. During our voyage we met headwinds which caused difficulty so that we arrived in this country in the autumn in the 7th lunar month[29], and we were received with due homage. In the **Dade** Epoch, year **dingyou**[30], in the sixth lunar month, we returned to our ship and sailed back. We arrived and anchored on the shore of **Siming**[31] on the 12th day of the 8th lunar month.

Even though I do not know all the details of their customs and the administrative matters of this country, I know enough general information and major matters.

Notes on: Introduction

(1) We should note at the outset that **Zhenla** (真臘) (**Tchenla**) or **Zhanla** (占臘) is strictly a name the Chinese (**Sui** dynasty, 6th century AD) called ancient Cambodia. The Khmers (Cambodians) never called their country by such a name. To the Khmers, the country was known at one time as Kōk Thlôrk, then Kampujadesa (8th century AD). Pelliot did extensive research in old Chinese records and in western publications about the origin and the meaning of **Zhenla**, and concluded that all explanations are simply unsubstantiated speculations. There has never been a Khmer record (stone inscription or otherwise) calling the Khmer country **Zhenla**. Ly Thiam Teng cited his discussion with Mr. **Zhang Shaoming**, a Chinese researcher on Far Eastern history who helped him to obtain the microfilm of **Zhou Daguan**'s Record (**Zhenla Feng Tu Ji**) in 1962. He suggested that **Zhenla** was derived from the Chinese word for pure beeswax. There are Chinese records that mentioned a country (in the area of present day Cambodia) where Chinese merchant ships used to go and buy beeswax to make candles. The Chinese 'Guide to the World States: Cambodia' (published by the 'Social Sciences Academic Press, **Beijing**, China, 2005') also mentioned the country **Zhenla**, where Chinese merchants bought

Fig. 00-01. Map sketch showing Zhou Daguan's trip by Chinese junk across the South China towards Cambodia.

honey and wax in ancient times. Beeswax and honey production was one of the important agricultural activities, as shown on two 11th century stone inscriptions (k.421 & k.913) of a royal order from King Udayadityavarman II, assigning districts to provide beeswax and honey (Malleret 1963).

(2) Khmer: "Kampuchea" (Cambodia).

(3) Tibetan Buddhist Holy Book (西番經): Pelliot did not doubt that the Tibetan lamas knew of Cambodia in the 13 century AD.

(4) According to **Jin Ronghua**, these overseas ports are those along the eastern coast of today's **Hainan** and other nearby islands.

(5) Seven-Islands Sea (**Qizhou Yang** 七洲洋) is a group of seven small islands about 60km northeast of **Hainan's** northeast coast. It is not the Paracel Islands as some people had thought (**Jin Ronghua** 1976) (Fig. 00-01).

(6) **Jiaozhi** Sea (交趾洋) is the area of the sea between the Gulf of Tonkin and the coast of today's Central Vietnam.

Fig. 00-02. Map sketch showing probable towns (marked with large red stars) Zhou Daguan had or had not seen (e.g. Pôsat) along Tonle Sap River on his way to Angkor. Ponley and Kampong Preah could be what Zhou called Banlu cun (半路村) [half-way village] and Fu cun (佛村) [Buddha village]. The red boundary represents the frontier of present day Cambodia.

(7) **Zhancheng** (占城) was Champa which covers today's central Vietnam. In Champa, **Zhou** stopped over at the port known today as Quinhon.

(8) **Zhenpu** (真蒲) is (according to Pelliot) in the Cap Saint-Jacques region or Baria in present day South Vietnam. It was the old Khmer province of "Preah Suorkièr".

(9) **Kunlun** Sea (崑崙洋) is the Poulo-Condor Sea (Pelliot), where there is a group of islands called Poulo Condor. The word Poulo Condor came from the Malay word pùlau = island, and cundur = gourd. The Khmer name is "Koh Trâlāch" meaning 'The Gourd Islands' (Tia Then 2005).

(10) The word **gang** (港) can mean port, river branch or estuary.

(11) White reeds - Most likely a mixture of the wild sugarcane (*Saccharum spontaneum*) (Khmer: "bâbos") and the giant cane (*Arundo donax*) (Khmer: "trèng"?) which grow along the edges of forests or on the banks of streams and rivers (Gangstad, et al. 1972).

(12) **Zhanan** (查南) is Kampong Chhnang City. "Kampong" = port; "chhnang" = pottery. Kampong Chhnang is the traditional center for pottery making. It is on the left bank of Tonle Sap River some 50km before it expands into a lake (Tonle Sap Lake).

(13) Half-Way Village = **Banlu Cun** (半路村) [**Ban** (半) = half, **lu** (路) = way/road, **cun** (村) = village]. **Zhou** could have descriptively referred to a village he had seen from the boat, or he could have transliterated the name of a village that had particular characteristics that made him remember, such as a fishing port for example. The modern day town of Ponley, at about 5km inland to the west of Tonle Sap River and about a quarter of the way from Kampong Chhnang to Angkor, could be **Zhou's Banlu Cun**. It is now one of the main fish trading exchanges for Tonle Sap Lake. We do not know when the name Ponley came into use, but since it is along Tonle Sap River on the way to Angkor, it is a candidate for speculation.

(14) Buddha Village = **Fu Cun** (佛村) [**Fu** (佛) = Buddha, **Cun** (村) = village]. We think it is located in the area of today's village of Kampong Preah, in the sub-district of Chhnok Tru at the entrance to Tonle Sap Lake (Narang and Groslier 2003, Suon Pheav 1999) (Figs. 00-02 to 00-04). There are ruins of two small Prasat dated around the end of 7th to the beginning of the 8th AD. Coedès, Pelliot and many

20th century scholars erroneously thought it probably was the town of Pôsat (French: Pursat). This makes no sense because:

a) Pôsat (Pursat) is more than 20km inland west of Tonle Sap Lake, so that **Zhou** could not possibly have seen it on his way to Angkor.

b) The Khmer spelling of the town of Pôsat (ពោធិ៍សាត់) has nothing to do with Buddha or Bodhisattva (ពោធិសត្វ). It is derived from "Pô" (ពោធិ៍ = Bodhi tree) and "rôsat (រសាត់) (to drift). The town's original name was Pô Rôsat. Through time, the name evolved and lost the word "rô" (cf. Preface). Now the town is known only as "Pô-sat" (Dictionnaire Cambodgien, 1967). The meaning of "Pôsat" and "Bodhisattva" are completely different. This is a good example of the Khmer homophone that can be a pitfall trap for non-Khmers. Unfortunately, some modern maps of Cambodia printed in Latinized Khmer words, show the town and the province of Pôsat as Pôthisat which means Buddha – this is an unfortunate, unwitting error.

(15) **Zhou Daguan** used the word **Dan Yang** (淡洋) meaning 'fresh water sea' which is Tonle Sap Lake.

(16) **Ganbang** (干傍) – is probably a transliteration of the Khmer word "kampong" that **Zhou** thought was the name of a place. He probably did not realize that "kampong" simply means 'port' or 'landing', since he did not use the character **gang** (港) = port. Normally, Cambodians (in a boat) would say 'we arrive at the kampong' or 'we go up (disembark) the kampong'. If they are embarking, they would say 'we go down the kampong'. On the other hand **Zhou's Ganbang** could be the present day floating village of Kampong Khleang, an ancient port on the norhern bank of Tonle Sap Lake during Angkor period (Narang Nouth 2011). From that port to Angkor is about 50km rather than 50 **li** as estimated by **Zhou** (Fig. 00-05).

(17) **li** (里) is a Chinese unit of distance, for practical purposes equal to 0.5km.

(18) A book, **Zhu Fanzhi** (諸番志) = 'Various Records on Foreign Countries' written by **Zhao Rushi** (趙汝適) in the Song dynasty in AD 1225.

(19) Modern **Panyu** or **Fanyu** (番禺) is a county in the **Guangdong** Province of China – this therefore does not make sense. Pelliot thought it must be an alteration or an error in reproducing the Record.

Fig. 00-03. Prasat Srey (right) and Prasat Pros (left) dated from the end of 7th to beginning of 8th century AD in Kampong Preah district; the small red roof was recently put to prevent rain water from flooding the tower (Photo S. Uk, 2013).

Fig. 00-04. Present day village of Chhnok Trou adjacent to Prasat Kampong Preah district (Photo S. Uk, 2013).

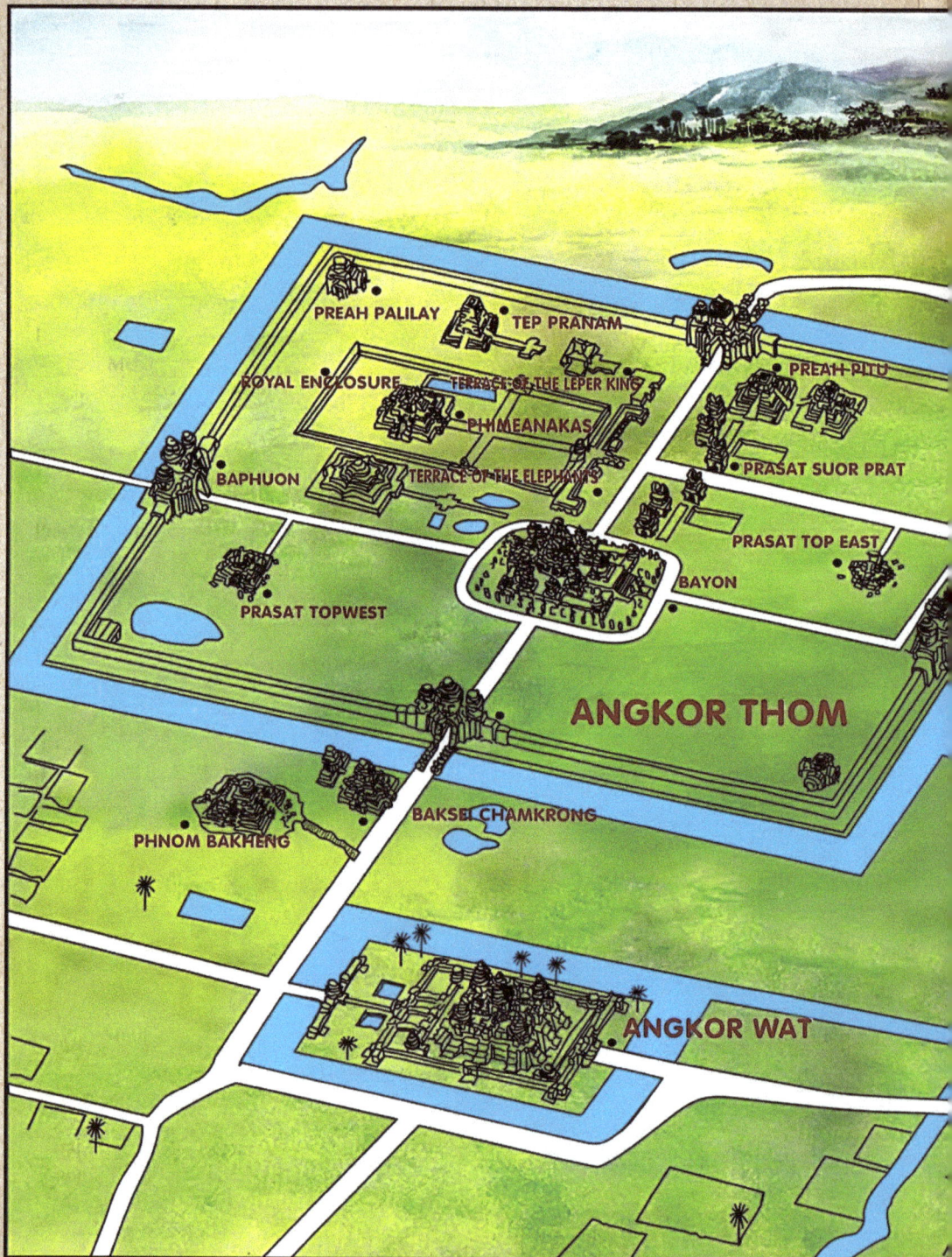

Fig. 00-05. Map sketch showing present day Angkor (Credit TourismCambodia.com).

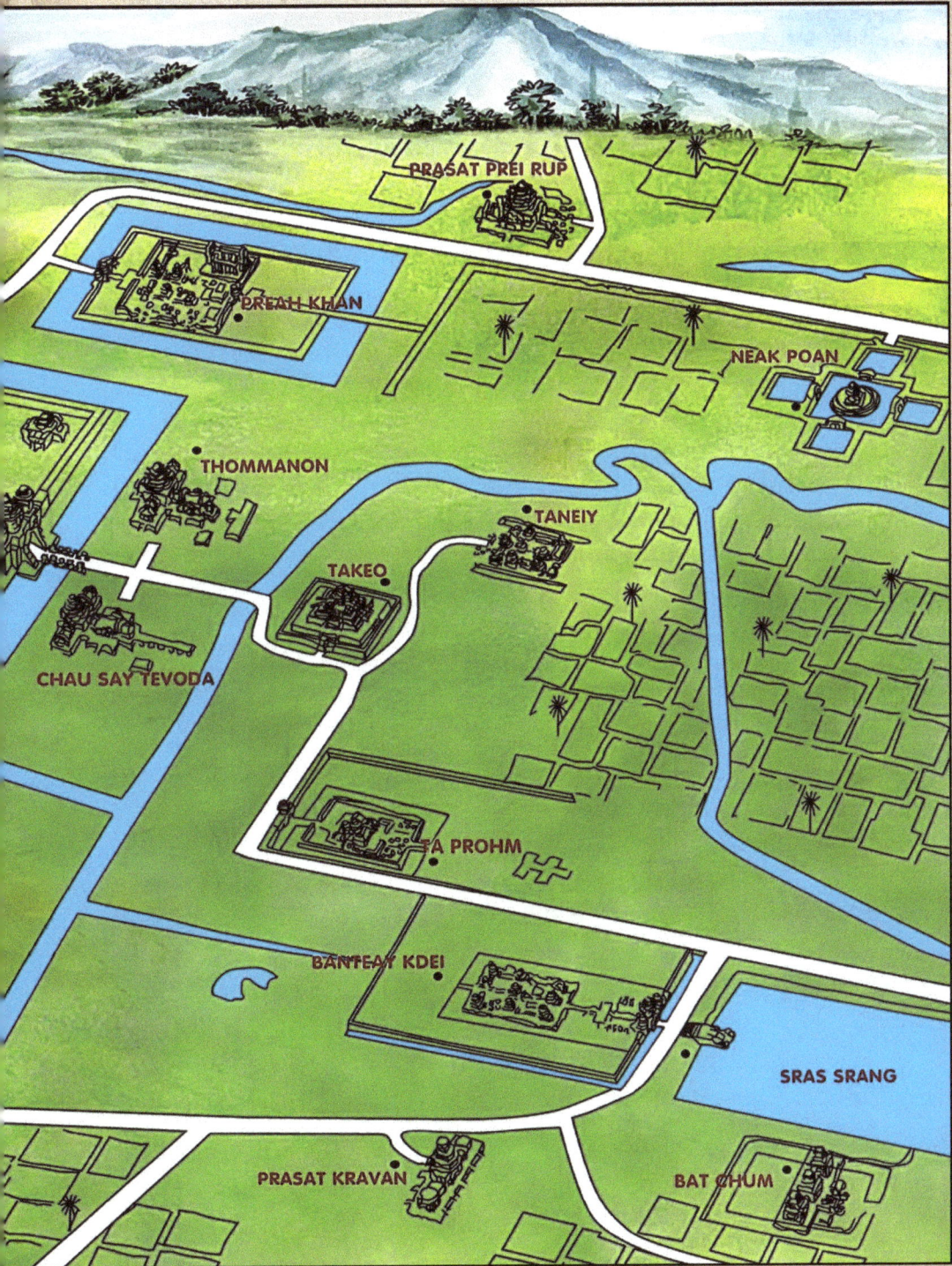

PRASAT PREI RUP

PREAH KHAN

NEAK POAN

THOMMANON

TANEIY

TAKEO

CHAU SAY TEVODA

TA PROHM

BANTEAY KDEI

SRAS SRANG

PRASAT KRAVAN

BAT CHUM

(20) **Zhou**, like most Far Eastern writers, often did not pay much attention to the accuracy of direction, geographical position, or dimensions (as can be seen later in his description). In this case, it should be southeast rather than east. Earlier, after entering the estuary, he mentioned 'we travelled northwards' rather than the actual direction 'north by northwest'.

(21) For Imperial China, 'Four Seas' meant the 'World'.

(22) The mentioning of Generalissimo **Suo Dou** (唆都) by **Zhou Daguan** is confusing. According to Maspero (1928) and Pelliot (1951) **Suo Duo** set up the Mongol administration of **Zhancheng** (Champa) in AD 1282 and died (decapitated) in fighting with the Annamites (Vietnamese) to the north of Champa some time in January/February 1285. **Zhou** seemed to have mixed up the mission of a **wanhu** (see below) named **He Zizhi** (何子志) and a **qianhu** (see below) named **Huang Fujiè** (皇甫傑) who were sent by the emperor to Siam rather than to **Zhenla**. When their ship stopped over in Champa, they were arrested and killed in February 1283.

(23) A **wanhu** (萬戶) is a general bearing a gold plate and a tiger insignia (虎符), and commands 10,000 soldiers.

(24) A **qianhu** (千戶) is a senior officer also bearing a gold plate but without insignia, and commands 1,000 soldiers.

(25) Year **yiwei** (乙未) is the first year of the **Yuanzhen** (元贞) epoch (AD 1295); year **bingshen** (丙申) is the second year (AD 1296).

(26) Holy Son of The Heaven = Emperor.

(27) In the **Yuan** dynasty, **Mingzhou** (明州) is today's **Ningbo** (寧波) in **Zhejiang** Province.

(28) **Wenzhou** (温州) in **Zhejiang** Province.

(29) Pelliot dated as 1 – 29 August, AD 1296.

(30) The first year of **Dade** (大德) epoch, year **dingyou** (丁酉) (AD 1297).

(31) Pelliot: **Siming** (四明) is another name for **Mingzhou** (modern **Ningbo**).

I
THE CITY PERIMETER

The city measures twenty **li** in circumference[1]. There are five gateways, each with double doors. Only the east side has two gateways, the rest have only one. The outside of the city wall is surrounded by a huge moat. Outside the moat there are passageways to large bridges. On both sides of each bridge, there are 54 large stone statues of divinities that look like military commanders. They are huge and mean-looking. The five gateways are similar. The balustrades of all the bridges are of stone, carved in the form of a snake. Each snake has nine-heads[2]. The arms of the 54 divinities hold onto the snake's body as if trying to pull it back to prevent it from running away. Over the gateways there are three[3] Buddha heads with faces looking to the four [cardinal] directions[4], and the one in the middle is gilded. On both sides of the gateways, there are carved stones in the form of elephants.

The city wall was constructed by piling stones one on top the other up to two **zhang** [about 7m] high. The stones are tightly constructed and very sturdy. No weeds can grow on the wall. However, there are no battlements[5] on the wall. Sugar palm trees[6] are planted on the inner side of the wall. Empty buildings[7] can be seen everywhere. The inside of the wall slopes downwards. It can be more than 10 **zhang** [about 33m] wide and has big gates in it. These gates open in the morning and close at night. There are also guards on duty. Dogs are not allowed to enter these gates. Criminals who have been sentenced by having had their toes cut off are also barred from entering. The city is quite square[8]. There is a stone tower in each of the four directions[9].

Fig. 01-01. Restored head of the right balustrade of the south gate of Angkor Thom. The neck stems supporting each head are labelled 1, 2, 3, 4 to the left and to the right of the central neck, which is labelled as 0 to suggest that the nāga has actually nine heads (Photo S. Uk, 1999). Garnier (1885) wrote: 'Un gigantesque dragon de pierre forme balustrade des deux côtés et vient redresser à l'entrée du pont ses neuf têtes en éventail.' Translation (S. Uk): 'A gigantic stone dragon forms a balustrade on each side lifting its nine heads up in the shape of a fan at the bridge entrance.' We beg interested archeologists to verify the real number of the nāga heads instead of accepting seven heads as generally believed. Compare the difference in design of the nāga head in Fig. 01-02.

Fig. 01-02. Right balustrade of the Victory Gate (East) of Angkor Thom with a 'seven-headed' nāga. The design of the nāga neck is different from that of the south gate (Photo S. Uk, 2011).

At the center of the city, there is a golden tower[10] surrounded by more than twenty stone towers, as well as more than one hundred stone chambers. On the eastern side, there is a golden bridge with two golden lions standing on the left and the right sides. There are rows of eight gold Buddha statues at the bases of the stone chambers. To the north of the golden tower at a little over one **li** [= 500m], there is a bronze tower[11] which is even taller than the golden tower and is a very impressive sight. Below this bronze tower, there are also more than ten stone chambers. Further north from this [bronze tower], another one **li** more, is the king's residence. In his private compound, there is another golden tower[12]. Maybe this is the reason why foreign merchants often talk about "the rich and noble **Zhenla**".

About half a **li** beyond the south gate is a stone tower[13], which, according to legend was built in one night by **Lu Ban**. The tomb of **Lu Ban**[14] is situated about one **li** from the south city gate. Its perimeter may reach ten **li** [= 5km], and it has several hundred stone chambers.

Fig. 01-03. 'Nine-headed' nāga in the lower half of the Underworld gallery of the Leper King's terrace (Photo S. Uk, 2005).

The east baray[15] is situated ten **li** from the east gate; its perimeter is one hundred **li**. There is a stone tower in it with stone chambers. In the tower, there is a reclining bronze Buddha[16]. There is often water flowing out of its navel.

The north baray is situated at five **li** north of the city. There is a square golden tower[17] with several dozen stone chambers. A golden Buddha, a golden lion, a bronze elephant, a bronze ox and a bronze horse are found here.

Fig. 01-04. Angkor Thom south gate surmounted by three towers. The biggest central tower has one face on each side looking north-south, the two smaller side-towers have one face each looking east-west. Similar to the four-faced towers of the Bayon, this symbolizes the king's power extending into the four cardinal directions of the universe (Glaize, 2003). There are indications of two wooden doors mounted one behind the other on each side of the entrance (what Zhou Daguan called the gate with two doors) (Photo S. Uk, 1999).

Fig. 01-05. The Khmer sugar palm trees (*Borassus flabellifer*) typical of the country side scenery of Cambodia (Photo S. Uk, 2006).

Fig. 01-06. Sculpture of a palmate-leaf palm on a bas-relief of Prasat Bayon (Photo S. Uk, 2005).

Notes on: 1. The City Perimeter

(1) The Chinese text in the title **cheng guo** (城郭) means 'city outline/ perimeter'. The city here refers to what is known today as Angkor Thom (Big City).

(2) Although Pelliot translated faithfully **Zhou's** word of 'nāga (snake) with nine heads', in his comments he categorically said that all the nāgas on the balustrades have only seven heads. Harris also thought the same. We disagree – we believe that the nāgas of the south gateway have nine heads. **Zhou Daguan** who lived in Angkor for almost one year, could not possibly have confused 9 with 7. Although all the balustrades on all the causeways into Angkor Thom are badly damaged, our proof of the nāga with nine heads is as follows:

a) In his 'Voyage d'Expedition en Indo-Chine' in 1866, Francis Garnier (1885) wrote – 'Un gigantesque dragon de pierre forme balustrade des deux côtés et vient redresser à l'entrée du pont ses neuf têtes en éventail...'. Translation (S. Uk): 'A gigantic stone dragon forms a balustrade on each side lifting its nine heads up in the shape of a fan at the bridge entrance:...'. Pelliot, meticulous as he was, seemed somehow to have missed this in Garnier's report.

b) If one examines closely each of the restored nāga heads on the south causeway balustrades, one can see the neck remnants of the two outer heads that make up nine heads (Fig. 01-01). Angkor sculptors had used five, or seven, or nine headed nāgas. For example, the nāgas on the balustrade of the Angkor Thom Victory Gate (East causeway) is of a different design and has only seven heads (Fig. 01-02). In the underworld gallery of the Leper King's terrace, there are carvings of 5-, 7-, and 9-headed nāgas (Fig. 01-03 shows a nine-headed nāga).

We beg interested archeologists to re-examine carefully all the nāga heads on all the five gates leading into Angkor Thom to confirm or refute our comments.

(3) Pelliot: Five Buddha heads. According to **Jin Ronghua**, the Chinese character for 3 (三), if not clearly written by hand, can be erroneously reproduced by a scribe as 5 (五). The gateway (gopura) is surmounted by three towers that **Zhou** called heads. The big center tower has two

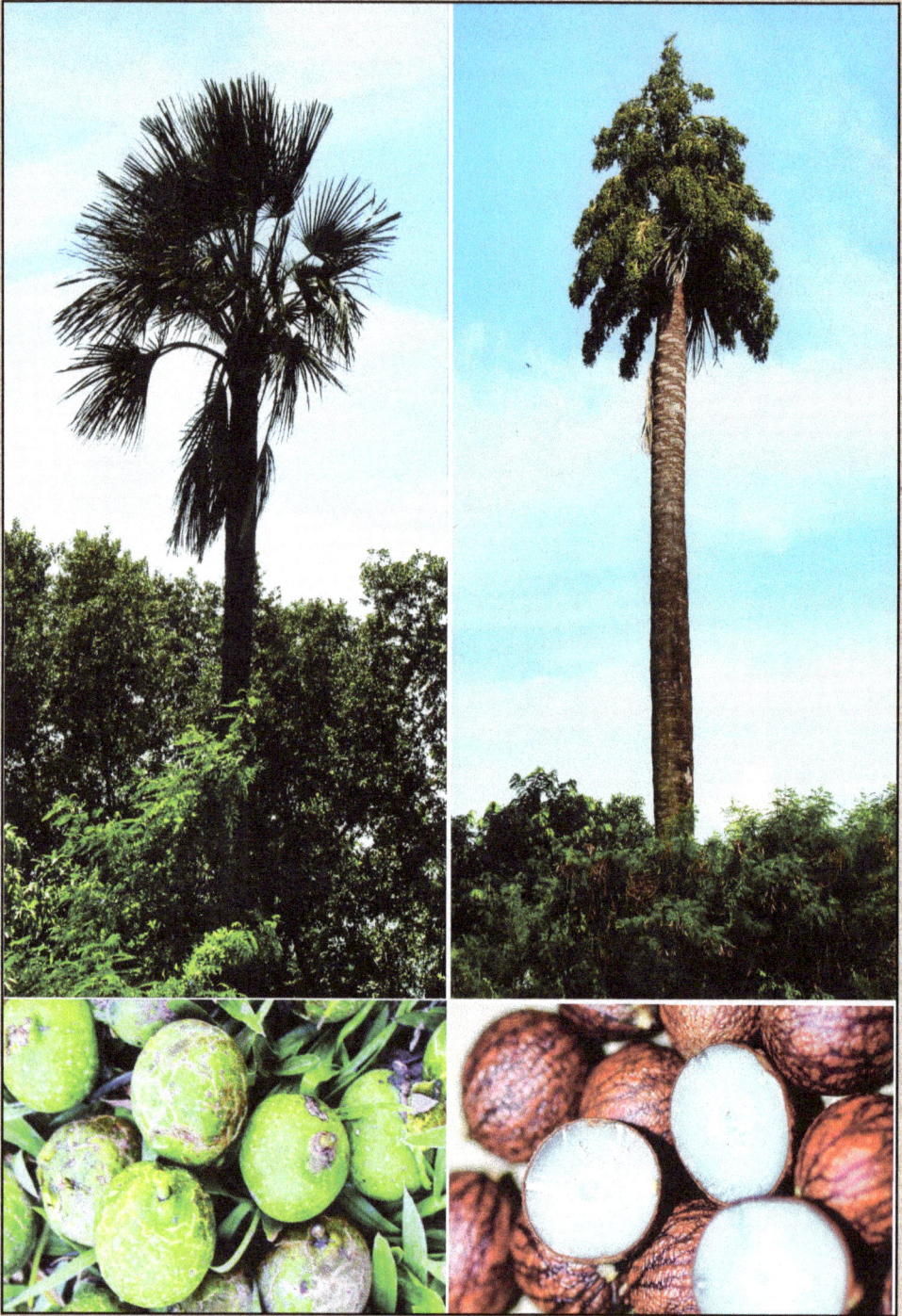

Fig. 01-07. *Corypha utan* palm. Mature tree about 30-40 years old (upper left). Fruiting tree about 70-years old (upper right). Young fruits (bottom left). Ripen fruits (bottom right) (Photo Nirano Tek, 2006).

faces, one on the north and one on the south side; the two smaller side-towers have one face each on the outside, one looking east, the other looking west (Fig. 01-04). These four faces looking towards the four cardinal directions symbolize (as the four-face towers of the Bayon) the king's power extending into the universe (Glaize 2003).

(4) The **Wu Guan** text has the character 西 for 'west' which could be erroneously copied by a scribe as 四 for 'four'; thus, it must be a script mistake.

(5) Battlements: The Chinese word **nüqiang** (女墙) literally means 'female wall' which is an additional layer on top of the main wall structure with small gaps for shooting out for defence purposes.

(6) Sugar palm: **Zhou** probably used the word **guanglang** (桄榔) to simply designate the 'sugar palm'. The most probable sugar palm he referred to would be the ubiquitous Khmer sugar palm, also known as Asian palmyra palm (*Borassus flabellifer*) that gives Cambodia its characteristic scenery. This palm was often mentioned in stone inscriptions (Dagens 2005) and carved on walls of monuments (Figs. 01-06 & 03-03).

a) **Guanglang** (桄榔) today is the Chinese common name for the sugar palm, *Arenga pinnata*. In Cambodia this palm species is rare but can occasionally be found in the Elephant Mountain range; it is not cultivated. In contrast to the Khmer sugar palm that has palmate leaves, *A. pinnata* has pinnate leaves (Dy Phon 2000).

b) Pelliot, after much self-debate, decided that **guanglang** (桄榔) was the sago palm (*Metroxylon rumphii*). Sago palm grows mainly in the swamps of the Indonesian archipelago and does not exist in Cambodia.

c) If **Zhou** meant the starch palm, it would be the species *Corypha utan* [Khmer: "doëm chraèr" (Fig. 01-07)] that produces starch in the trunk like the sago palm (cf. Johnson 1992); *C. utan* also has palmate leaves, whereas the sago palm has pinnate leaves. Some *C. utan* trees can still be found in Kampong Thom Province adjacent to Siem Reap Province (where Angkor is), or possibly in Siem Reap Province itself. Currently the largest concentration of trees grown for starch flour (Khmer: "m'sauv chraèr") are found mostly in "Saāng Koh Thom" area south of Phnom-Penh. In Cambodia, "m'sauv chraèr" is used mainly for making sweets. It is unlikely that **Zhou** was referring to starch palm since he used the word **guanglang** (桄榔) that means sugar palm.

Fig. 01-08. Prasat Bayon in the Angkor Thom compound (Photo S. Uk, 2005).

Fig. 01-09. Prasat Baphuon in the Angkor Thom compound (Photo S. Uk, 2006).

d) Not to be confused with the well known sago starch (that is produced from the sago palm), is a local Khmer "sagu" flour ("m'sauv sagu"). Note the spelling difference between "sago" and "sagu". The Khmer "sagu" is the arrowroot plant (*Maranta arundinacea*) widely grown in Cambodia for starch, or simply to be eaten boiled like sweet potato. This Khmer name maybe the cause of confusion for Pelliot.

(7) Those empty buildings could be the wooden structures reserved for the guards on duty.

(8) The city wall is not exactly square. Only the two eastern corners have right angles, whereas the angle of the north-west corner is acute and the south-west corner is obtuse (Marchal 1928).

(9) **Zhou** loosely used the words 'four directions'; in fact, each of the stone towers is on the inside of each of the four corners of the city wall. They are now known as Prasat Chrung = Corner Towers (Giteau 1974).

(10) Prasat Bayon, built by King Jayavarman VII to house a huge Buddha statue as a symbol representing the cult of Devaraja (Coedès 1961, Dumarçay 1973, Groslier 1973) (Fig. 01-08).

(11) Pelliot, Smithies, and Harris: Prasat Baphuon (Fig. 01-09).

(12) Prasat Phimeanakas (Celestial Palace) built towards the end of 8th century AD (Dagens 2005) as a symbolic representation of the sacred Mount Meru (of the Hindu mythology) to house the cult of Devaraja (Coedès 1961).

(13) **Zhou's** stone tower is Phnom Bakheng (Fig. 01-10). It is situated on top of a 70m high hill 400m south of Angkor Thom's south gate (not at 0.5 **li** = 250m as **Zhou** mentioned). It was built by King Yaśovarman I around AD 900 at the center of his capital city, Yaśodharapura. The legend **Zhou** heard that it was built overnight by the Chinese mythical architect **Lu Ban** is strange. The story is similar to the Khmer legend about Angkor Wat being built by "Preah Visnukar" (the celestial engineer) in one night (cf. Preface). However, this legend about Angkor Wat seems to be more recent than **Zhou Daguan**'s time and could be inspired by the latter's legend of Phnom Bakheng.

Fig. 01-10. Top of Prasat Phnom Bakheng mentioned by Zhou Daguan as being built in one night by Lu Ban (Photo S. Uk, 2001).

Fig. 01-11. Prasat Angkor Wat (Zhou Daguan's Tomb of Lu Ban) viewed on the spring equinox from the causeway just after the western entrance on 21 March 2006 (Photo S. Uk).

Fig. 01-12. Prasat West Mebon in West Baray (before complete dismantling possibly for anastylosis where the reclining bronze Vishnu statue was found (Photo S. Uk, 2001).

Fig. 01-13. Prasat Neak Pean in the middle of Zhou Daguan's North Baray (Photo S. Uk, 1999).

(14) Pelliot: Prasat Angkor Wat (Fig. 01-11). It is puzzling that **Zhou** referred to the temple of Angkor Wat as **Lu Ban**'s tomb. **Lu Ban** was a Chinese carpenter, inventor, engineer and philosopher in the 5th century BC. He attained the mythical status of the god for construction and is responsible for some of the most amazing architecture, particularly the design of dragon motifs in ancient temples. He is thus equivalent to the Khmer concept of Preah Vishnukar. It is also surprising why **Zhou** did not write about Angkor Wat more than simply mentioning that "it has more than 100 stone chambers". When **Zhou** arrived in Cambodia, Angkor Wat was already more than 170 years old. Maybe people at the time considered it as just a tomb for a long gone king, or because its towers were not golden, it did not attract **Zhou's** interest as other monuments did. It is also possible that as a foreigner, **Zhou** had no free access to the temple. Angkor Wat was positively identified as the mausoleum of King Suryavarman II who had the posthumous name of Paramavishnuloka (He who had entered the heavenly world of Vishnu).

(15) Baray is an artificial water reservoir. According to Pelliot it should be the west baray (see note 16). **Jin Ronghua**: the discrepancy is not clear.

(16) The reclining bronze Buddha is in fact the statue of Visnu that was found in the west baray (Jacques 1990) and not the East Baray as **Zhou** mentioned. **Zhou** gave the dimensions of the baray (whether the East or the West Baray) as roughly ten times bigger than they actually were.

(17) Jayataka Baray built by Jayavarman VII surrounding Prasat 'Neak Pean' (Fig. 01-13).

2
PALACE AND HOUSING

The palace, the houses of officials and the mansions all face east. The palace is situated to the north of the golden tower and the golden bridge, and near to the north gate. Its perimeter[1] is about five to six **li** [about 2.5-3.0km]. The tiles covering the central tower are made of lead. The tiles for the rest of the buildings are made of clay, yellow in color. The lintels[2] and columns are huge, all with carved or painted figures of Buddha. The buildings are rather majestic. The long galleries and many passageways of various lengths and levels give an impression of scale. In the chamber where the king conducts the state affairs, there is a golden window. On the left and the right side [of the window] there are square columns supporting about 40 to 50 panes of mirrors. The base of the window is carved in the form of elephants. I have heard that there are many marvellous places inside the palace, but the strict ban prevents me from having a look inside.

I was told by the locals that the king goes up to sleep inside the golden tower[3] every night. Inside there is a nine-headed snake spirit[4] that is the lord of the land for the whole country, and is in the form of a woman. Every night she sees the king first, sleeps and couples with him. Even the queen would not dare go in. The king leaves at the 'second drum beat'. Only then can the king sleep with the queen or with the royal concubines. If the snake spirit does not appear one night, the time of death for the king has arrived. If the barbarian king fails to go up one night, then disaster will certainly happen.

The housing systems for members of the royal family and high functionaries are vastly different from those of the ordinary people. Their houses are covered with thatch, only the family temples and the principal bedrooms are allowed tiles. The size of the house must be built according to the official rank of the owners.

As for the houses of the common folk, only thatch is used; one dares not use tiles. Although the size of the house can suit one's wealth, one never dares to imitate the houses of high officials.

Fig. 02-01. Entrance to the Royal Palace in Angkor Thom complex (Photo S. Uk, 2001).

Fig. 02-02. The king in audience (South gallery of Angkor Wat) (Photo S. Uk, 2001).

Notes on: 2. Palace and Housing

(1) The dimensions given by **Zhou** are about twice the actual size of the palace ground. It is a normal error for a visual estimate of an area, particularly when there are many buildings. Furthermore, Chinese as well as Cambodian writers are not normally precise about dimensions and numbers.

(2) Lintels: The original text **qiao** (橋) means bridge. **Jin Ronghua** and **Xia Nai** changed to **liang** (樑) which means lintel.

(3) Prasat Phimeanakas (Celestial palace) built as a symbolic temple-mountain with a shrine at the top (Fig. 02-03).

Fig. 02-03. Prasat Phimeanakas with its top shrine where the king allegedly spent every evening with a nagi (female snake) in the form of a woman (Photo S. Uk, 1999).

(4) The story of the king sleeping with the nāgi (female snake) spirit is a legend that must have circulated for centuries. It could have originated in India or from rumours that Cambodians often like to invent. The truth will never be known. **Zhou** himself said that the story was told to him by the locals.

This story of the king and the snake is another example of myth and truth being mingled in some episodes of Khmer history. Prasat Phimeanakas (Celestial Palace) with its shrine at the top (Higham 2001), symbolized the heart of the Khmer power under the reign of many Angkor kings (Schweyer 2004). Thach Toan (2009) suggested that it is a chapel suitable for a king to meditate in and to pay homage to Queen Somà, the founder of Cambodia and the Angkorian dynasty. According to legend she was the daughter of the king of nāgas (mythical snakes), ruler of the ocean world.

The shrine at the top of Phimeanakas appears to be a private royal chapel inside the palace ground (Jacques 1990 and Glaize 2003).

3
CLOTHING AND JEWELRY

Everyone, from the king down to ordinary men and women wears their hair in a bun, leaves the body bare and wraps only a piece of cloth round the waist. To go out, one adds a large piece of cloth to wrap around the normal small piece. The cloth has various grades. That of the king is worth three to four **liang**[1] [about 90-125g] of gold and is very luxurious and brilliant. Although people in this country know how to weave, they also import fabrics from Siam and Champa. Usually, the fabrics from 'western ocean' countries are considered the best quality. They are very fine and delicate.

Only the king can wear cloth with a floral pattern all over. On his head he wears a golden crown similar to that worn by **Jingang**[2]. Sometimes the king does not wear a crown, but only a string of threaded fragrant flowers such as jasmine wound around his hair bun. Around his neck, he wears big pearls weighing more than three **jin**[3] [1.5kg]. He also wears gold bracelets on his arms and ankles and rings on all his fingers. All rings are set with cat's-eye gemstones. He is bare-footed. The palms and the soles are dyed red. Every time the king comes out, he carries a golden sword. As for the ordinary people, only women can have their palms and soles dyed red, men dare not do so. The royal family and high officials can wear fabric with patterns of a few widely spaced flowers, the ordinary officials can only use fabric with patterns at each end. For the commoner, only women can wear fabric of the latter kind. The newly arrived Chinese, even if they wear cloth with patterned ends, are not accused of a crime because they are considered as the people who do not know the custom; they are called **an ding basha**[4] meaning 'those who do not know the rules'.

Notes on: 3. Clothing and Jewelry

(1) **Liang** is a Chinese unit of weight = 50g, 1 old **liang** ≈ 31g

(2) **Jin Ronghua: Jingang** (金剛) is a divinity guarding the entrance to the temple, standing holding a chest-high club known as a vajra in Hindu and Buddhist religions.

(3) Chinese unit of weight - (one **jin** = 500g)

(4) **an ding basha** (暗丁八殺): The text is most likely a distorted Chinese transliteration of the Khmer words "ât" (**an** 暗) = do not, "doëng" (**ding** 丁) = 'know' and "phiësā" (**basha** 八殺) = 'language'. Thus **an ding basha** = do not know the language.

Fig. 03-01. Royal women (Bayon bas-relief) (Photo S. Uk, 2006).

Fig. 03-02. Royal women portrayed in the South Gallery of Angkor Wat (Photo Kent Davis).

Fig. 03-03. Women attending a ceremony – their hair in a bun, their bodies bare and their waist wrapped with a piece of cloth (Bayon bas-relief). Also there is a sculpture that appears to be a sugar palm tree (Photo S. Uk, 2006).

4
OFFICIALS

This country has ministers, generals and astronomers. Below these are various lower ranking officials [as in China], but they have different names. Most of these officials are royal relatives; otherwise one has to marry into royalty by offering a daughter as a concubine.

When out and about, the officials are recognized by their insignia and accompanying staff according to their ranks. The highest rank uses a golden palanquin and four parasols with golden handles. The next rank uses a golden palanquin with two parasols with golden handles, then a golden palanquin with one parasol with a golden handle. When only one parasol with a golden handle is used, it is of an even lower rank. Below these, only one parasol with a silver handle is used. There are some who use silver palanquins. The officials who use parasols with golden handles are called **bading**[1] or **anding**[2]. The ranks that use parasols with silver handles are called **siladi**[3]. The parasols are all made of red silk with the flounces hanging almost to the ground. The normal oil-treated[4] parasols are covered with green silk; their flounces are shorter.

Notes on: 4. Officials

(1) **Bading** (巴丁) = "mrateng" = High official title in ancient Khmer, somewhat equivalent to 'Lord'.

(2) **Anding** (暗丁) - Evolution of "mrateng" => "âm-mdaèng" in modern Khmer.

(3) **Siladi** (厮辣的) may be the Chinese transliteration of "sarathéi" (សារថី), a Khmer word of Sanskrit/Pali origin meaning 'carriage driver' or 'horse trainer'; the official title "raja sarathéi" = 'royal horse trainer' or 'royal carriage driver' (Dictionnaire Cambodgien 1967). Coedès suggested the word śreṣthin (an official title), but this is an unknown word in Khmer.

(4) Normally treated with tung oil.

Fig. 04-01. Low ranking official riding on elephant, as recognized by the presence of a single parasol as mentioned by Zhou (Bayon bas-relief) (Photo S. Uk, 2006).

5
THE THREE RELIGIONS

Scholars are called **banjie**[1], Buddhist monks **zhugu**[2] and ascetics **basiwei**[3].

I do not know what is the **banjie's** philosophical base. There is no such thing as a school or teaching establishment. It is also difficult to find out what books they read. I see these people wearing clothes like the ordinary folk except they hang one strand of white thread around their necks to indicate that they are scholars. The **banjie** who go to serve in the government, usually attain high positions. The thread around their necks remains all their life.

As for the Buddhist monks, they shave their heads and wear yellow robes leaving the right shoulder bare. They tie a yellow cotton skirt around their waists and walk barefoot. The temples are allowed roof tiles; in the center there is only one Buddha statue that looks like the Sakyamuni[4] Buddha and is called **bolai**[5]. It is dressed in red, moulded from clay, and painted with colors. There is no other statue but this one. The faces of the Buddha statues in the towers are all different; all are cast in bronze, and there are no bells, drums, cymbals, flags, canopies or other things. All the monks eat fish and meat, but do not drink wine. The food offerings to the Buddha also contain fish and meat. The monks eat one meal a day. The food is taken from families who offer it to them. There is no kitchen in the temple. The dharmas that the monks recite are many. They are written on palm leaves packed together very neatly. The monks write black words on the leaves. They do not use a brush or china ink. I do not know what tool[6] they use to write. The monks also use palanquins and parasols with gold or silver handles. The king consults the monks on major state matters. There are however, no nuns in the temples.

The ascetics, **basiwei**, dress like the ordinary people, but wear a head cloth white or red in color similar to the Tartar Mongol women's **gugu**[7] but only a bit shorter. These ascetics have hermitages[8] like the Buddhist temples but smaller. Asceticism is not as popular as Buddhism. They worship a piece of

Fig. 05-01. Early 20th century Khmer writings on talipot palm leaves (Photo S. Uk, 2005).

stone[9] similar to the altar stone in the Chinese temple for the Earth God. I do not know the origin and the way they practice their belief. There are female members, and the hermitages are also allowed to have roof tiles. The **basiwei** do not take food from others, do not let others see them eating, and do not drink alcohol either. I have never witnessed an ascetic reciting religious texts or doing things for the benefit of others.

The boys of the ordinary people who need education are sent to Buddhist monks for learning and become monks themselves. Later when they are older, they return to the laic life. I am not able to check any further detail about this.

Fig. 05-02. Young talipot palm (*Corypha umbraculifera*) with its central new leaf shoot (about 3m tall). For writing purposes, the shoot is cut just before it opens into the fan shaped leaf, trimmed to the required sizes and dried slowly in rooms protected from sunlight (Photo Nirano Tek, 2006).

Fig. 05-03. Scholars reading scriptures on palm leaves (Bayon bas-relief) (Photo S. Uk, 2005).

Notes on: 5. The Three Religions

(1) **Banjie** (班诘) is the transliteration of the Khmer word "pândit" meaning a 'learned person', i.e. a scholar known as a Brahman. The Brahmans occupied high positions in the royal court. In present day Cambodia, the Brahmans are known as Bakou and serve as official keepers of the royal heritage in Phnom-Penh (Dagens 2005). Their position in the royal court is hereditary. They tie their relatively short hair into a small bun. When presiding over royal rites such as a coronation or a king's birthday, they wear a white sampot (somewhat similar to the Indian dhoti worn by Mahatma Gandhi), a white straight necked jacket and a sacral white thread around their necks similar to the old description by **Zhou Daguan**. The name Bakou is derived from the Pali word "barkū" meaning the Brahman who has achieved the knowledge of the Veda (the oldest Sanskrit scripture in Hinduism).

(2) **Zhugu** (苧姑) is the transliteration of an ancient Khmer word "chau kov" meaning 'director' or for Buddhist monks, 'abbot' (Dictionnaire Cambodgien 1967). The word is still used in Thailand for the title of Buddhist monks.

(3) **Basiwei** (八思惟) must be **Zhou's** transliteration of Khmer "bâswi" which is derived from the Sanskrit "tapasvin" = ascetic (Ly Thiam Teng 1971), a person who practices strict self-denial and abstinence from worldly pleasures. Pelliot and Harris translated **daozhe** (道者) as 'followers of the **dao**' which could be mistaken for people who practice Chinese Taoism.

(4) The most common statue that represents the enlightened Siddharta Gautama as the Sakyamuni Buddha.

(5) **Bolai** (孛賴) is the Chinese transliteration of the Khmer word "Preah". The Chinese characters are monosyllabic and cannot transliterate the Khmer sound of the double consonant 'pr' in "Preah"; the result is Bolai. "Preah" is of Sanskrit origin and means 'superior', 'magnificent', 'praiseworthy'. In Cambodia, it is used as a prefix for Buddha, Buddhist monks and kings.

Fig. 05-04. Three ascetics with cylindrical head caps facing ordinary people in a ceremony (Bayon bas-relief) (Photo S. Uk, 2005).

Fig. 05-05. Śivalinga worship symbol of Śivaism (Bayon bas-relief) (Photo S. Uk, 2005).

(6) A metal stylus is used to write on specially prepared pre-cut strips of leaves of talipot palm (*Corypha umbraculifera*, synonym *C. lecomtei*); the scored leaves are then rubbed with mashed henna to bring out the black writing (Figs. 05-01 & 05-02). Talipot palm grows wild in the semi-dense forests of Cambodia and the rest of the Indochinese Peninsula. To make the palm-leaf book (Khmer: Sātrā sloek rīt), the young palm bud is cut before the leaflets open. The leaf veins are carefully removed and the leaflets, still bound together in a block, are trimmed to the required sizes. The trimmed leaf blocks are then left to dry slowly under a press in a ventilated room protected from sunlight. It should not be confused with the leaves of the ubiquitous domestic Khmer sugar palm of the genus *Borassus flabellifer*. The leaflets of the latter are not sufficiently long and wide for use in document writing. Furthermore, when dry they are brittle and not resilient enough to be kept as books for long periods. They are used mainly for roofing.

(7) **Jin Ronghua: gugu** (罟姑) is a cylindrical crown sometimes decorated with feathers, pearls and precious stones, and can reach two to three **chi** (about 70-100cm) high. The ascetic's headdress must be similar to the scuptures on many bas-reliefs of the various temples representing the ascetics with beards and cylindrical head caps (Figs. 05-03 & 05-04).

(8) The Chinese text **gongguan** (宮觀) means temple. In modern Cambodia (up to the 1960s), the Buddhist ascetics (no longer Śivaists) were still known as "tabâhs" (tapasvin) or rishi. To be away from wordly pleasures, they live alone in isolated small wooden hermitages in the forests.

(9) The stone must be the linga, symbol of Śivaism (Fig. 05-05).

6
THE PEOPLE

The southern barbarians are known as coarse, ugly and very black. It is not realized that this is true for the inhabitants of the islands, remote villages, alleys and lanes [of towns]. As for the palace ladies and **nanpeng**[1] - women from noble families – most have skin as white as white jade. This is because they do not see sunlight. Normally, all women and men wear nothing other than a piece of cloth wrapped around their waists. They leave their breasts bare, their hair rolled in buns. They walk bare-foot. This is also true even for the king's wives.

The king has five wives, one principal wife and four others representing the four cardinal directions. Below these, I have heard that there are three to five thousand concubines and maids. They also separate themselves into ranks and rarely go out. Every time I entered the royal palace, I saw the king always coming out with the principal wife and sitting at the golden window in the principal room. The palace ladies all lined up according to their ranks in the two galleries below the window. They tried to lean [on the windows] to peek. I was able to see them.

When a family has a daughter with beauty, she will certainly be summoned to the palace. Below these, the women who come and go to serve in the palace are called **chenjialan**[2]. There are no less than one to two thousand and all have husbands and live and mix with the ordinary people. They shave their hair a bit above their foreheads somewhat similar to the northerners' 'open waterway'[3]. They mark their foreheads with vermilion as well as both of their temples. This is the sign identifying the **chenjialan**. Only these women can enter the palace. The others below them cannot get in. In front and behind the inner palace, there are many of these women [**chenjialan**] walking along the passages and alleys. The ordinary women wear their hair in buns but without hairpins, combs, or head and face ornaments. However, they wear gold bracelets on their arms and gold rings on the fingers. In fact the **chenjialan** and other palace women all wear these. Both men and women often wear perfume mixed from sandalwood, musk and other scents.

Fig. 06-01. Ancient Chinese sketch of a Khmer woman and man [after the Chinese Encyclopedia Si ku quan shu (四庫全書) in the Qing dynasty (清)].

All families practice Buddhism.

In this country there are many transvestites[4] who go out in groups of ten or more each day all over the market places often with the intention of attracting the attention of the Chinese to get fat rewards. It is really disgraceful and disgusting.

Notes on: 6. The People

---

(1) **Nanpeng** (南棚) must be the transliteration of a Khmer word that cannot be identified, but **Zhou** gave its meaning in the text as women from noble families.

(2) **Chenjialan** (陳家蘭) is possibly a transliteration of an unidentified Khmer word. Pelliot did not translate it and questioned the suggestion by Coedès that it is the transliteration of the Sanskrit "śrngāra" that is equivalent to the modern Khmer word "sröngkiër". **Zhou's** description that those women are servants of the palace fits the modern Khmer word "srey snâm", the women who take care of the palace services in organized shifts (Dictionnaire Cambodgien 1967).

(3) **Jin Ronghua**: Among the northern Chinese in the **Yuan** Dynasty, the Manchurians shaved their heads about 6cm in from the forehead. This looks like an 'opening waterway' (**kai shui dao** 開水道). Maybe **Zhou** was referring to this hair style.

(4) The original Chinese words **er xing ren** (二形人) literally means 'two-form person' anatomically speaking. Zhou's text implies that their behaviour is like male prostitutes. We decided to translate it as transvestites on the basis that **Zhou** could recognize those people only from their clothes and make up.

7
WOMEN GIVING BIRTH

After giving birth, the native women take hot cooked rice mixed with salt and put it into their private orifice. Normally after one day and one night they remove it. This practice is to prevent disease and to shrink [their intimate organ] to make it like a virgin's again. When I heard of this for the first time I was surprised and was deeply suspicious about this information. However, in the family I stayed with, there was a woman who gave birth, so I know this fact very well. One day after the birth, this woman carried the baby to bathe together in the river, which is really strange. Every time I meet people they always tell me that the native women are highly lustful. Only one or two days after childbirth, they would couple with their husbands. If a husband did not satisfy the wife's desire, then he could be abandoned like the case of **Maichen**[1]. If the husband has to work far away, he can only be absent for a few nights. After more than 10 nights, the wife would surely say "I'm not a ghost, how can I sleep alone?". Their sexual desire is very strong. However, I have also heard that some women remain truly faithful.

Women age very quickly because they marry and give birth too young. Those of 20 or 30 years of age look like 40 or 50 year old Chinese women.

Notes on: 7. Women Giving Birth

(1) **Maichen** (買臣), surname **Zhu** (朱), was a poor Chinese scholar in the **Han** dynasty, who earned his living by chopping and selling firewood. For 20 years he was unable to provide a decent living for his family. So his wife left him. Later he was appointed as an official in the government, and his wife committed suicide. Pelliot noted that he died in 116 BC.

Fig. 07-01. A woman giving birth (Bayon bas-relief) (Photo S. Uk, 2005).

8

MAIDENS

When a girl is born into a family, her father and mother are bound to bless her by saying: "May you in future, be loved and have hundreds and thousands of husbands"[1]. A Buddhist monk or an ascetic must be invited to deflower the girl from the age of six to nine for the rich families and at eleven for the poor. This is called **zhentan**[2].

Every year, the government authority chooses one day [in the month] corresponding to the 4th Chinese month and makes it known to the whole country. The girl's parents who plan the **zhentan** must apply to the authorities beforehand and the latter would give a big candle marked with a notch. At the appointed night, when the candle burns to the notch, it is time for **zhentan**.

One month, or two weeks, or ten days before the date, the parents must choose and reserve a monk or an ascetic depending on where temples and hermitages are located. Often, the temples also have their own clientèle. The renowned and good monks would all be reserved in advance by the families of high officials or the rich, whereas the poor have no choice. The families of the officials or the rich offer the monk wine, rice, fabric, betel, and silver goods up to one hundred **dan**[3] and worth around no less than two to three hundred **liang** [about 6-9 kg] of Chinese silver[4]. Those with less wealth still offer thirty to forty, or ten to twenty **dan**. Therefore, the poor families must wait until the girl is eleven years old before having this ceremony because of the difficulty in providing these offerings. There are people who give money for poor girls' **zhentan**. This is so called "doing good deeds". In one year a monk can only perform this ceremony for one girl. Once a monk has accepted an engagement, he no longer can serve another one.

On the night of this ceremony, the family set up a big banquet of food, drink, and drum music to receive relations and neighbors. They build a high platform with a canopy to display clay models of people and animals, sometimes more than ten, sometimes only three or four. The poor families do not display any. They are all based on a certain story. After seven days they dismantle them.

Fig. 08-01. A man carrying a dan (擔) (Khmer: "âmraèk") of goods (Bayon bas-relief) (Photo S. Uk, 2005).

On this evening just after dark, they go to welcome the monk with the palanquin, parasol and drum music, and bring him back. They use colorful silk to knot and build two pavilions, one for the girl to sit in and the other for the monk. I do not know what the monk says. The drums and music sound very loud. This night people are allowed to make a lot of noise without restriction. I have heard that when the time comes, the monk and the girl go inside the room. The monk uses his hand to take away her 'virginity'[5], and puts it into wine. Some say that the girl's parents, relatives and neighbours each dab [the wine] on their foreheads or taste it with their mouths. Some say that the monk couples with the girl at this time, but others say he does not. People do not let the Chinese see it, so I do not know the real truth.

When the day is just about to break, the palanquin with parasol and drum music comes again to take the monk back. Afterwards, gifts such as cloth and silk have to be used to buy back the girl from the monk, otherwise she will still belong to him all her life and cannot marry anyone.

I witnessed this affair on the 6th night of the 4th month of year **dingyou** in the **Dade** Epoch[6]. Before this ceremony, father and mother always sleep with their daughter. After this, the girl is excluded from the parents' room, and can go anywhere she wishes without being watched and restricted. As for the marriage, although the parents receive money as a gift, it is very simply done. It is common that many men have sex with the girls first and marry them later. In their custom, this is considered neither shameful nor strange.

On the night of the **zhentan**, sometimes in one alleyway there are up to ten houses holding this ceremony. In the town there are many groups of people criss-crossing the passageways to collect monks and ascetics. There is not a place where one cannot hear the sounds of the drums and music.

Notes on: 8. Maidens

---

(1) Simply a common traditional Khmer blessing that the girl will be liked or loved by many potential suitors – The expression 'hundreds and thousands of husbands' should not be taken literally.

(2) **Zhentan** (陣毯). There is no logical explanation for this word. It is neither a Chinese word nor a Chinese transliteration of a Khmer word. There is no record of this custom in Cambodia from ancient stone inscriptions or from recent documents. Many scholars have presented different explanations and speculations, but none are satisfactory.

(3) **Dan** (擔) can mean the unit of weight equivalent to about 50kg, or it can mean the load in two normally cylindrical containers that one person can carry on the shoulder with a pole or a yoke (Fig. 08-01). The latter meaning seems more likely, considering the gifts of up to 100 **dans**; if it were weight, it would be 5 tons – a rather exaggerated amount.

(4) The original text said 'Chinese white gold', but **Jin Ronghua** changed it to 'Chinese silver'.

(5) Pelliot translated as 'deflower' the girl. The Chinese words literally mean 'take out her child status'. Although the boisterous ceremony as described by **Zhou Daguan** must have taken place, the custom of 'deflowering the girl' in Cambodia was never known and **Zhou** himself admitted that he could not find out the truth since Chinese people are not allowed to witness the ceremony. It is hard to believe that the Buddhist monks and the ascetics who practice strict abstinence from worldly pleasures should deflower the girls. On the other hand, monks or ascetics could perform the animistic tradition that the Khmer continue to practice together with Hinduism and Buddhism as they still do today.

(6) Year **dingyou** (丁酉) is the first year of the **Dade** Epoch (AD 1297).

9
SLAVES

For household slaves, all people buy the 'wild' men for their services. Some have more than one hundred. Those who have less have ten to twenty. The very poor have none.

The wild people are native mountain dwellers. These people are of different races and tribes[1], and are commonly called **Zhuang**[2] thieves. They come to the city and dare not wander in and out of their masters' houses. In a quarrel, when one [a Khmer] calls the other '**zhuang**', it means that he really hates the other so much as to feel it in the marrow of his bones. This shows how these [**zhuang**] people are looked down upon. The young strong ones can be sold for one hundred copper coins[3], the old weak ones are worth only thirty or forty. These people are allowed to sit and sleep only on the ground floor[4]. They are allowed to go up into the house only when they are needed for service and they must kneel, join hands together and prostrate themselves before they dare enter the house. They call the master **batuo**, the mistress **mi**; **batuo**[5] means father, **mi**[6] means mother. If they make a mistake and are beaten for it, they would bend their heads down, accept the beating and dare not move at all.

The males and females mate among themselves. The master would never have reason to have [sexual] contact with them. If a Chinese who comes here and has been a long time without [sex], he is not choosy; once he has had relations [with one of these females] and the master hears about it, the next day he would not sit with the Chinese because he had coupled with a wild one. If a slave has intercourse with someone outside the household, gets pregnant and gives birth to a child, the master would not question the matter even though it is improper. He will profit from the birth because the child will become his slave in the future. If a slave runs away and gets caught, he/she would be tattooed blue on the face, and be restrained by wearing a metal lock around his/her neck, or sometimes between his/her arms and legs.

Notes on: 9. Slaves

(1) In Cambodia there are at least ten tribes of native mountain dwellers. The **Zhuang** (Khmer: "Choang") belongs to the "Stieng" group of natives which includes four tribes - the "Choang", the "Kuoy", the "Rodê" and the "Samrê".

(2) **Zhuang** (撞) is the Chinese transliteration of the Khmer word: "choang". Nowadays, the word "choang" is still used to insult people as in **Zhou Daguan's** time.

(3) **Zhou** used the word **bu** (布) that means the ancient Chinese copper coin used in the **Yuan** dynasty (**Jin Ronghua** 1976; Chinese-English dictionary 1979). Maybe people used the real Chinese coins or maybe some sort of copper pieces were minted locally. All Westerners (Pelliot, Aschmoneit, Smithies, Harris) translated **bu** as the piece of fabric used for trading in place of money.

Fig. 09-01. Traditional Khmer house on stilts (Photo S. Uk, 2005).

(4) Traditional Khmer houses are built on stilts with open space underneath. The ground floor is actually the ground underneath the main house (Fig. 09-01).

(5) **Batuo** (巴馳) must be the transliteration of Khmer "bétôr" or "bédôr", from Pali "béti" = father. Now the term is used only in memorial ceremonies for royal ancestors. Modern Khmer uses "bétār or "bédār" = father for royalty or literary writing, and "pa" or "öw" = father, or "maè" = mother, for commoners (Dictionnàire Cambodgien 1967).

(6) **Mi** (米) is possibly misheard or erroneously transliterated by **Zhou Daguan**, since in Khmer, mother is called "maè" which is derived from "mé" meaning 'female leader' (Narang and Groslier 2003). In modern Khmer, "mi" is a vernacular term used (sometimes in a friendly manner or sometimes impolite) to address girls or young women; it is not related etymologically to the word "mé".

10

LANGUAGE

This country has its own language. Even though the sounds are very similar, the people of Champa and Siam cannot speak or understand it. For example: one is pronounced **mei**[1], two **bie**, three **bei**, four **ban**, five **bolan**[2], six **bolan mei**, seven **bolan bie**, eight **bolan bei**, nine **bolan ban**, and ten **da**[3]. The father is called **batuo**[4]. The paternal uncles are also called **batuo**. The mother is called **mi**[5], and the paternal and maternal aunts and 'elderly' women neighbours are also called **mi**. Older brothers are called **bang**; older sisters are also called **bang**. Younger brothers are called **buwen**. The maternal uncle is called **chilai**[6] whereas the husband of the paternal aunt is called **bólai**[7].

They reverse the order of words - for example when we say "this man is **Zhang san**'s[8] younger brother", they would say "**buwen Zhang san**"; "that man is **Li si**'s maternal uncle", they would say "**chilai Li si**". They call China "**Beishi**", an official "**bading**", a learned man "**banjie**". So they do not call the Chinese official "**Beishi bading**", but "**bading Beishi**". They do not call the Chinese learned man[9] "**Beishi banjie**", but "**banjie Beishi**". It is all more or less so. This is the general outline. Concerning the high officials, they speak their official style, the scholars their own style of scholarly expressions; the monks or ascetics also each have their own language. The city people and villagers also have different ways of speaking. This is not different from China.

Notes on: 10. Language

(1) Khmer pronunciation: 1 = muëy, 2 = pi, 3 = béi, 4 = buën, 5 = pram.

(2) **Bolan** is the transliteration of "pram" = 5 resulting from the Chinese inability to pronounce 'R' that ends up as 'L', and the ending 'M' as 'N'. This is true for all subsequent composites of **bolan**, e.g., 6 = **bolan mei**, 7 = **bolan bie** [pram pi], 8 = **bolan bei** [pram béi], 9 = **bolan ban** [pram buën].

(3) **Da** is "dâb" = 10.

(4) **Batuo** (巴馳) is the Khmer word "bétôr/bédôr", from Pali "béti" = father. Now the term is used only in memorial ceremonies for royal ancestors. Modern Khmer uses "bétār/bédār" = father for royalty or literary writing (Dictionnaire Cambodgien 1967).

(5) Possibly misheard or erroneously transliterated by **Zhou** since in Khmer, mother is "maè", but aunts are called "mīng" (as well as all non-related older women as a form of politeness).

(6) **Chilai** (吃賴) maybe the transliteration of the 10th century Khmer word "khlai" meaning 'brother or sister-in-law' (Pou 2004) which evolved into the modern Khmer "thlai" meaning 'in-laws' (Coedès 1989). Maybe **Zhou** misunderstood the information about the maternal uncle that he called **chilai**.

(7) By the same token, **bólai** must be the Chinese transliteration of "pū thlai" = uncle-in-law. In Khmer, "pū" means 'uncle'. In modern Khmer, the word "pū" can mean the maternal uncle, or the mother's younger brother-in-law, or the father's younger brother-in-law, or the mother's and father's male cousins.

(8) **Zhang san** (張三) literally means the third boy born to the **Zhang**'s family and **Li si** (李四) means the fourth boy to the **Li**'s family. However, this saying does not refer to a specific **Zhang** or **Li** family, rather it is just a popular expression like the saying – the Smiths keeping up with the Joneses. For the Cambodian social interactions, a person is always addressed with a prefix word such as 'older brother' so-and-so, or 'younger sister', 'aunt', etc.

(9) **Xiucai** (秀才) translates as 'a learned man'. He can be a scholar or one who has passed the imperial examination at the county level in China.

II
WILD MEN

There are two types of primitive[1] tribes. One type knows the common language and is sold in cities as slaves. The other type is unteachable and does not know the language. These people do not live in houses. They wander with their family members on mountain tops. They carry a clay pan[2]. If they meet a wild animal, they shoot it with an arrow or strike it with a spear. After killing the animal, they make fire by striking stone, cook, eat together, then move on.

These people are very cruel; their poisons are very potent; they often kill each other in their own group. In the nearby flat areas, some cultivate cardamom and kapok[3] and weave cloth. The cloth is thick and coarse with unusual patterns.

Notes on: 11. Wild Men

(1) The word **yĕ** (野) means wild or primitive in the same sense as wild plants, and in this case, 'Primitive tribal people'. **Zhou** could be talking about any of the native tribes that may include the Stieng, Kuoy, Rhade, Jarai, Krung, etc.

(2) The Chinese text has no punctuation, i.e., no equivalent of comma (,) or fullstop (.). If the sentence is cut after 'mountain top' (**shan tou** 山頭) (**Jin Ronghua**), the text has the meaning as translated above. On the other hand if the sentence is cut just after 'mountain' (山) (**Xia Nai**) leaving the word 'top' (頭) to the next sentence, the text would then read 'they wander with their family members in the mountains. They carry (wear) a clay pan on their heads'.

(3) The original Chinese writing **mumian** (木綿) must refer to **mumian** (木棉) that means kapok (*Ceiba pentandra*) because the first **mian** (綿) bears no relationship to kapok tree. This **mian** (綿) is the waste silk after the good fibres have been taken out by spinning. The characters 棉 and 綿 have the same pronunciation '**mian**'. Pelliot translated them as cotton tree. Kapok fibre is too short and too weak to be spun into yarn

Fig. 11-01. Giant *Tetrameles nudiflora* tree (a different plant family from kapok) with its huge spreading roots gripping the wall of Prasat Ta Prohm (Photo S. Uk, 1999).

to make cloth. However, during World War II some people in Touk Meas (in southern Cambodia) did wear coarse cloths made from kapok fiber due to the shortage of textile materials. Thus, **Zhou Daguan**'s description as thick (coarse) cloth has relevance. Smithies believes that 'kapok tree' is more correct. In the present day, kapok fiber is used for stuffing mattresses and pillows. The botanical name for kapok tree is *Ceiba pentandra* (Khmer: "kôor"). This grows to 4–15m in height. This is not to be confused with the species *Tetrameles nudiflora* (Khmer: "spuëng") that grows to huge heights (15-30m) and has gigantic roots above the ground, which grip the walls of Prasat Ta Prohm and Prasat Preah Khan in Angkor with devastating effects on the monuments (compare Fig. 11-01 with Fig. 11-02).

Fig. 11-02. A fruiting kapok tree (*Ceiba pentandra*) along a street in Phnom-Penh (about 8m in height) (Photo S. Uk, 2004).

12
WRITING

Common writings as well as official documents are written on deer skin or other hide that has been dyed black. The skin is cut into large or small, wide or narrow pieces according to one's wishes. Using a kind of powder similar to Chinese chalk, they mould it into small sticks named **suo**[1], hold this stick in the hand and draw on the skin to form the words. These words never come off. After writing, the person inserts the **suo** onto the top of his ear. From the shape of the letters, one can recognize who has written them. To remove the writing, something wet must be used. Mostly the writing has a similar appearance to that of **Huihu**[2] words. All documents are written from back to front[3] and not from top to bottom. I have heard **Yexian Haiya**[4] saying that the words sound somewhat like that of Mongolian. Only two or three words are different.

Earlier, they had no seals. When people need to bring complaints to the court, there are also no[5] writing shops to write for them.

Notes on: 12. Writing

(1) **Suo** (梭): **Zhou**'s description looks like the modern chalk stick made from calcium sulphate (Khmer: "déi sâ"), but the writing with modern chalk is easily erasable. It could be the chalk made from soft limestone that makes indelible marks on parchment. As a schoolboy during World War II when things were scarce, I used a piece of this limestone (from a nearby mountain) as writing chalk on slate board.

(2) **Huihu** (回鶻) = **Uygur** (維吾爾), a race in western China (**Xinjiang** Province). Khmer writing is derived from an alphabet of Southern India whereas the **Uygur** language is of Turkic origin, and the writing is in vertical columns, though from left to right and bear little resemblance to that of the Khmer. Why **Zhou** likened the Khmer to the **Uygur** language is not clear to me as a Cambodian – maybe because the two languages are so very different from Chinese.

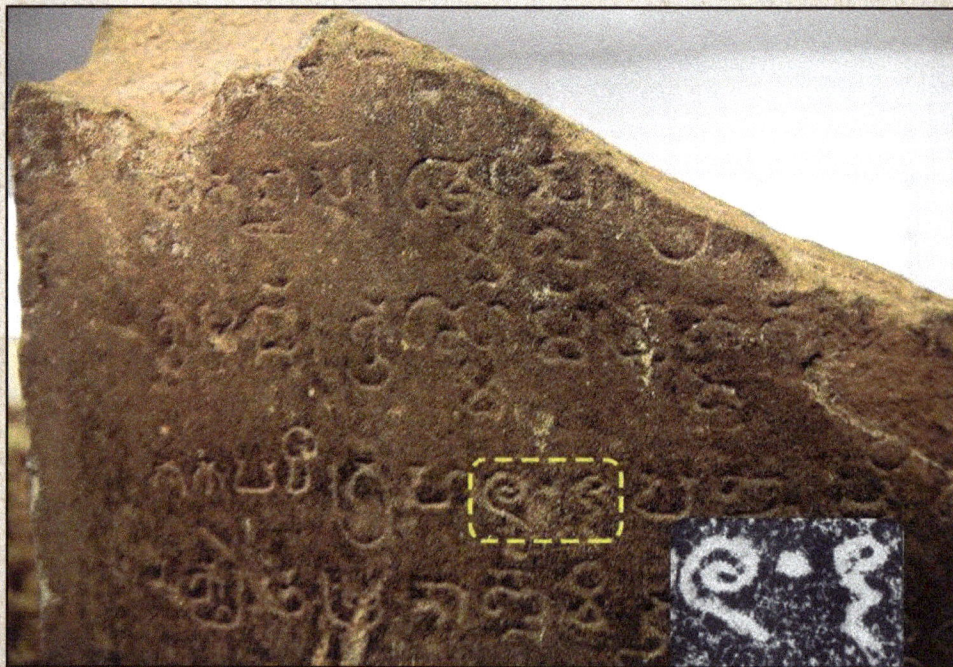

Fig. 12-01. Sample of pre-Angkor Khmer script from K-127 of Sambaur in Kratié province with highlighted numeral 605 (A. Aczel 2015). (Courtesy A. Aczel, Photo credit Mrs. Debra Gross Aczel, 2013).

(3) The Chinese writing is normally from top to bottom in columns from right to left and the pages follow the same order, whereas the Khmer writing is from left to right in horizontal rows from top to bottom with the pages going from left to right – to Zhou, this is writing from back to front.

(4) **Yexian Haiya** (也先海牙) = **Yexian** (也先), a Mongolian surname, maybe that of his travelling companion. Again **Zhou** and **Yexian**'s imaginations seem somewhat stretched. Samples of old Khmer writing from different periods are shown on Figs. 12-01 and 12-02. Prof. A. Aczel (2015) uncovered that the first physical numeral *zero* originated in the Khmer empire. The stone inscription K-127 with number 605 indicates the çaka year that corresponds to AD 683 (605+78). Thanks to Prof. Aczel, stele K-127 will be on display at the National Museum in Phnom Penh. As Cambodian, I am most grateful for his tireless effort.

(5) The original **Wu Guan** text said '…there are also writing shops…'. **Jin Ronghua** argued that since the previous sentence 'Earlier they had no seals', logically the negative should follow in the succeeding sentence, and he added the word <u>no</u> to read '…there are also no writing shops…'.

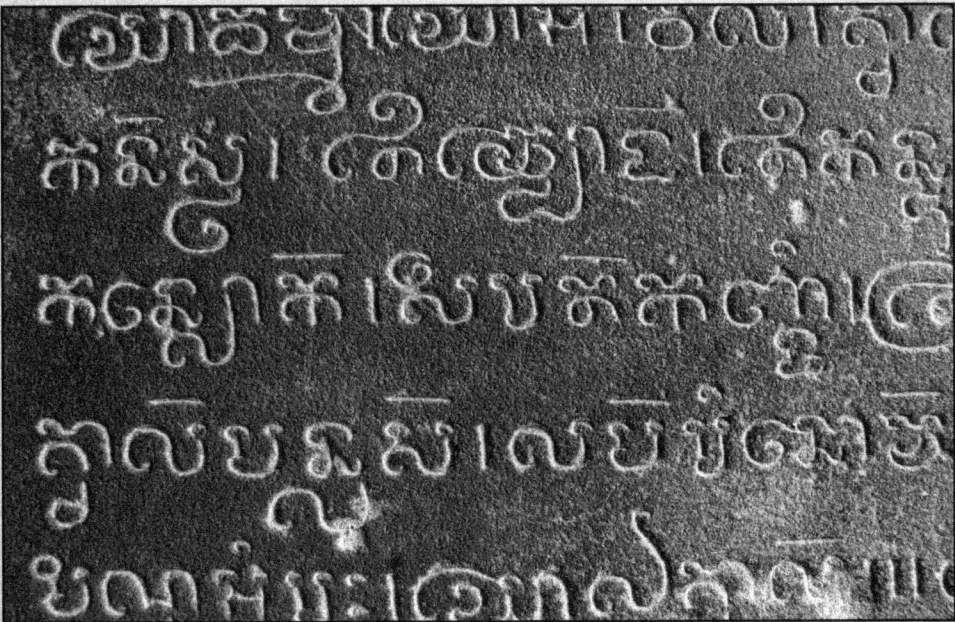

Fig. 12-02. Sample of Angkor period Khmer script on stone on the main door of Prasat Krâvan (Photo S. Uk, 2006).

13
NEW YEAR AND
CALENDAR ORDER

The 10th Chinese month is taken as the first month and is called **jiade**[1]. In front of the palace they build a big canopy with hanging lanterns and flowers; it can hold more than one thousand people. On the other side twenty **zhang**[2] [about 70m] away, they build high platforms with wooden poles tied together like bamboo scaffolding[3] used to build a **ta**[4]. These could be more than twenty **zhang** high. Each night, they build three or four, or five or six of these high platforms and put fireworks and rockets on them. These are done by the various districts and official houses. At nightfall, the king is invited to come out to watch the fireworks and rockets. These fireworks can be seen from one hundred **li** away. The firecrackers are as big as cannonballs[5] and their explosions so loud as to shake the whole city. The officials, their families as well as the nobility, each contribute giant candles and betel/areca nuts, and the expenses are rather large. The king also invites foreign delegates to spectate. This event can last half a month.

There is also one festival every month[6]. For example in the 4th month they throw the balls[7]. In the 9th month they celebrate **yalie**[8]. In this festival, all the people from the entire country come to parade in front of the royal palace. In the 5th month, they then 'Welcome Buddha Water'. People from far and near from the whole country collect Buddha water[9] and offer it to the king to wash himself. Then they row the boat on dry land; the king climbs onto a platform to watch. The 7th month has the 'burning the rice'[10]. The freshly ripened paddy is received outside the south gate and burned as an offering to Buddha. Many women come on carts or elephants to see this event, but the king does not come out to watch it. The 8th month is the **ailan**[11], the dancing festival. Dancers and musicians (Figs. 13-01, 13-02) are appointed to come into the palace to dance every day. Furthermore, there are pig fights (Fig 13-03) and elephant fights. The king also invites foreign diplomats to attend. This lasts ten days. As for other months, I cannot remember in detail.

Fig. 13-01. Angkorian musician and dancers (Bayon-bas relief) (Photo S. Uk, 2001).

In this country there are also people who know astronomy. They can calculate solar and lunar eclipses. The days of the long and short months are not the same as those of China. Our 13-month year corresponds to their 13-month year. In the year with an intercalary month, one month is also added. Their intercalary month is always the 9th month, but I do not know this in detail[12]. The night is divided into four[13] watches. Every seven days forms one cycle like the so called **kai bi jian chu** cycle[14] in China. The people in this country have no family name and no given name. They do not record the date of birth either. Most of them take the day of birth as their name. According to their belief, there are two best days, three average days, and two very bad days. Which day one can go eastwards and which day one can go westwards – even women know how to work it out. The 12 animal symbols of the cycle are also the same as in China, but they are differently named. For example, they call the horse, **busai**, the rooster, **man**, the pig, **zhilu**, and the ox, **ge**, etc. [15]

Fig. 13-02. Angkorian harpist (Bayon bas-relief) (Photo S. Uk, 2001).

Fig. 13-03. Pig fight (Bayon bas-relief) (Photo S. Uk, 2001).

Notes on: 13. New Year and Calendar Order

(1) **Jiade** (佳得): As elaborated by Pelliot, it is the Chinese transliteration of the Khmer "Kâdëk" (Sanskrit: Kārttika) in the Khmer lunisolar calendar which corresponds to the Chinese 10th month and starts in late October of the Gregorian calendar. It was a month of great religious festival in the 10th and 12th centuries AD (Pou 2004). In **Zhou Daguan**'s time, the year began in Kārttika (October-November) as supported by a mid 10th century inscription (Dagens 2005). The first month of the year seems to have changed from time to time. Often, the month Chaitra (March-April) of the lunisolar calendar marked the beginning of the year. The lunisolar calendar followed the Hindu tradition, but with local variations. To this day, some regions in India celebrate New Year at the beginning of the month Chaitra, others at the beginning of Kārttika. From the Angkor period to the present day, Cambodia uses both the lunisolar and the solar calendar. The current solar calendar corresponds to the Gregorian system, but the months are named differently (see Appendix B). Currently, the first month of the Khmer lunisolar calendar is "Mégasir" (Sanskrit: Mārgaśīrṣa) which falls in late November.

Regarding the New Year's celebration, **Zhou** might have confused it with the Kārttika festival because other inscriptions from the middle of the 10th century AD clearly mentioned two different celebrations on two different dates, one for the New Year, the other for Kārttika (Dagens 2005). However, Tum (2008) made calculations based on the Khmer lunar system back to AD 1000 and found that **Zhou**'s month of Kārttika is in fact "Mégasir", the present day first month of the Khmer lunar calendar (Kārttika being the 12th month). Currently, the celebration in Kārttika is the Water Festival (boat racing) which is the biggest festival of the year. Another important celebration mentioned in inscriptions is the spring equinox (21-24 March) in the month of Chaitra (Khmer: "Chèt"). Apparently, this spring equinox celebration was the New Year celebration in the 12th century at the time Angkor Wat was built (Mannika 1996). Nowadays, the New Year festival takes place in the month of Chaitra, but the exact time the New Year begins is adjusted to fall on a day between 12th and 14th April on the Gregorian calendar. It is based on the alignment of a star relative to the Sun and the Earth (Tum 2008). The time and the day when the New Year begins is calculated and officially published every year by the royal astrologer.

(2) One **zhang** (丈) = 10 **chi** (尺) = 3.3 m.

(3) **Pu gan** (撲竿): **pu** (撲) = to throw oneself forward or to touch lightly (this word is out of context in **Zhou**'s text); **gan** (竿) = pole, stick. According to **Jin Ronghua**, **pu** (撲) could be a writing mistake for the closely similar shaped character for **yang** (樣) = form, shape, style. Thus, the original **pu gan** should in fact be **yang gan**. This refers to the wooden poles (small tree trunks) that look like the bamboo poles which are normally used in China for scaffolding. Cambodia does not have big, straight bamboos as in China; thus, small, straight tree trunks are used for scaffolding in contrast to China where bamboos are used.

(4) The word **ta** (塔) refers to a tall construction that can be a Chinese pagoda, a stupa, a tower (e.g. a water tower), or a lighthouse.

(5) Although true cannonballs did not exist in the 13th century, the Chinese text refers to a projectile from a big weapon. We translate it as 'cannonballs' to make it more explicitly descriptive.

(6) In modern times, most of the monthly festivals mentioned by **Zhou** take place in the month of Chaitra during the New Year celebrations, e.g., the festivals of 'ball throwing', 'Buddha washing', and 'dancing', with local variations according to the regions of Cambodia (Porée-Maspéro 195?).

(7) A ball called "chhūng" in Khmer, made from a rolled up cotton scarf called "krâmār".

(8) Pelliot: census, register.

(9) The festival of 'Washing Buddha' is still practiced today during the Khmer New Year in the month of Chaitra (April) which is one month later than **Zhou Daguan**'s description. In all the Buddhist pagodas throughout Cambodia, the ceremony involves washing Buddha statues (large and small) with water scented with jasmine or roses. The wash water is then collected and offered to relatives for rinsing the body to bring health and good luck. The devotees wash the abbots and afterwards, the elderly people. We think **Zhou**'s text means 'gather the Buddha wash water' rather than the 'Buddha statues' since big statues cannot be brought to Angkor from all over the country without tremendous difficulty and effort.

(10) The festival of 'burning the rice' is now celebrated on the day of the full moon of the month of Māgha (3rd month of the lunisolar calendar).

(11) **Ailan** (挨藍): Pelliot debated on **'ailan'** or 'ngai lan'. The Chinese language does not have equivalent Khmer sounds for "ng", "r"; and "m". Thus, the most probable transliterated Khmer words would be "ngay râm" meaning 'dance day'.

(12) The current 8th month (Asādh) of the Khmer lunisolar calendar falls in June-July of the Gregorian calendar. Cambodia always inserts a 9th month after the month of Asādh in a repeating cycle of every second and third year. In China the intercalary years follow a similar repeating cycle, but the intercalary month is moved one month each time. This is why **Zhou** noted that the Khmer intercalary month is the 9th month only, and he does not know in detail why it is so.

(13) Pelliot: five, with a question mark.

(14) **Kai bi jian chu** (開閉建除), etc., is the jargon of Chinese astrology and fortune-telling. It is based on a cycle of twelve deities, six good and six bad (**Jin Ronghua** 1971). One should avoid certain days to do certain things such as making a business deal, buying a house, etc. Cambodians have a similar belief (even now), but based on a different system of calculation.

(15) Khmer years: horse = "sèhs"; rooster = "moën"; pig = "chrūk"; ox = "kô", etc.

14

DISPUTES AND LITIGATION

Even trivial disputes among the ordinary people are brought to the king for judgement. I was told that at the beginning there was no punishment by beating with bamboo sticks, but only fines. Also when the crime is serious, the convict will not be executed by hanging or decapitation. He is simply put into a pit which is dug outside the west gate and then filled up firmly with earth and stones. That is all. In other cases, criminals have their fingers or toes and for some, their noses cut off.

Adultery and gambling are not forbidden. If the husband knows of the wife's adultery, he would take two pieces of wood, tie them to the feet of his wife's lover and twist them so tight as to cause pain too excruciating for the latter to endure. He [the adulterer] has to give up everything he owns in order to gain his freedom. There are also cases of frame-ups with intention to swindle.

If anyone finds a dead man at the house gate, he would tie the body with a rope and drag it himself to a wilderness outside the city. There is no such thing as an inquest or body examination.

If a thief is caught, he can be detained or beaten by the people who catch him. There is also one remarkable way that can be used - if someone has lost something and suspects a certain person of theft, and this suspect refuses to confess, he is ordered to dip his hand into a frying pan full of very hot oil. If he is guilty his hand would be burned and ruined, if he is not, the skin and the flesh would be as before. This is the method used by those barbarians.

Also there is another case of dispute between two men when one cannot tell who is right or who is wrong. Then they do the following: on the other side of the palace, there are twelve small stone towers[1]. Each man is ordered to sit in one of these towers. Each is watched by the other family members from the outside. After one, two, three, or four days, the one who is in the wrong would certainly show symptoms. He comes out with boils or sores on his body, or with a cough and fever, or the like. The person who is in the right would have no bad thing happen to him. This method of

Fig. 14-01. Two of the twelve Prasat "Neang dâb bi" (Twelve Maidens Towers) also known as Prasat "Suor Proat" (Photo S. Uk, 2006).

judgement is called celestial court[2]. They can do it this way because the land spirit has this power.

Notes on: 14. Disputes and Litigation

(1) The twelve stone towers are outside the palace across the courtyard in front of the Elephant Terrace. They are known as Prasat "Neang dâb bi" (Twelve Maidens) or Prasat "Suor Proat" (Fig. 14-01).

(2) The Chinese word literally means 'celestial prison'.

15
ILLNESSES AND SKIN DISEASES

Generally, when people in this country are ill, they immerse themselves in water and wash their head repeatedly; they will naturally cure themselves. Many people of this country have skin diseases[1] and one can see them on the streets. The locals do not mind even to sleep or eat with them. Some say that the climate causes these diseases. It is said that the king also has such a disease[2]; that is why normal people do not despise this condition much. In my humble opinion, it is often caused by bathing after copulation. I have heard that the locals, both men and women, would go down to bathe immediately after just having satisfied their sexual desire. They catch dysentery that causes death in eight or nine cases out of every ten.

There are also medicines on the market, but different from the Chinese ones. I do not know what these are. Also there are some kinds of shamans who perform sorcery, which is rather ridiculous.

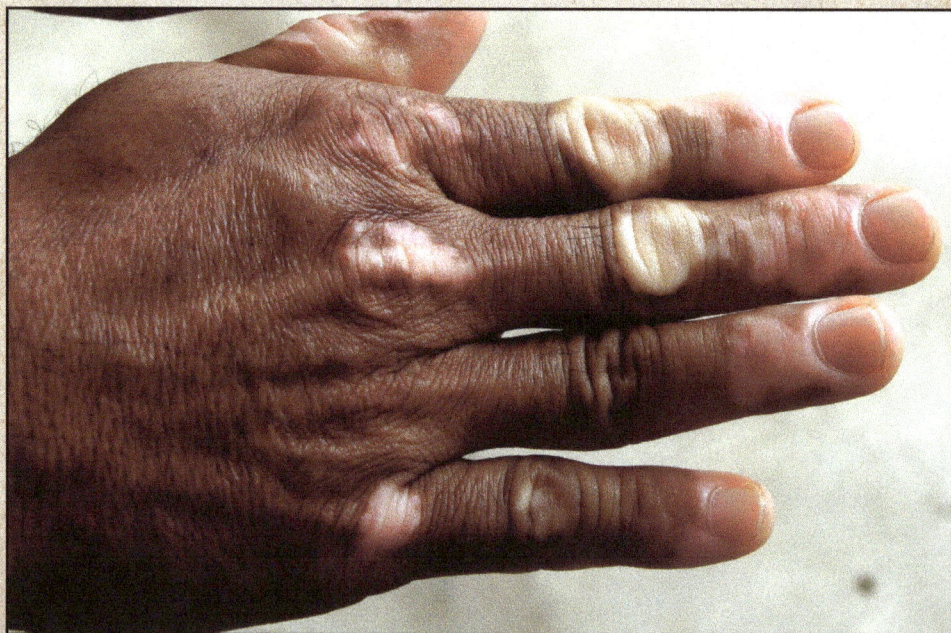

Fig. 15-01. A vitiligo hand of a Khmer from a Phnom Penh suburb (Photo Nirano Tek, 2015).

Fig. 15-02. Vitiligo
on the body of a rural
Khmer (Photo Im
Chhanna, 2015).

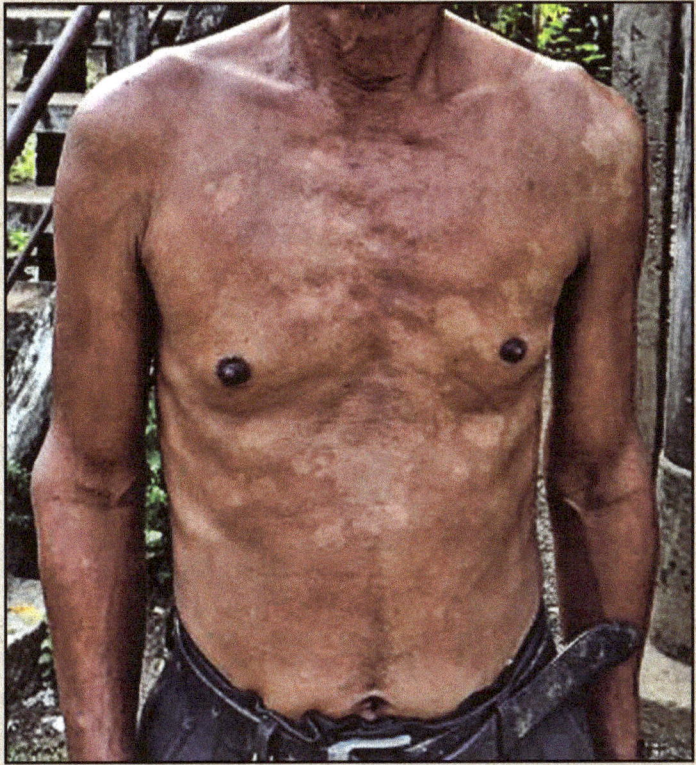

Fig. 15-03. According to a legend Preah Thong fights with a giant snake who is in fact
his father-in-law in disguise (Bayon bas-relief) (Photo S. Uk, 2011).

Notes on: 15. Illnesses and Skin Diseases

(1) We and Ly Thiam Teng (1973) disagree with the translation of **binglai** (病癩) as 'Diseases and Leprosy' by Pelliot (in French), Smithies (in English), Aschmoneit (in German), and Harris (in English). Leprosy causes disfigurement or loss of limbs, and it is not logical that leprous people would be seen so widely on the streets in the city. **Bing** (病) = illness, disease. **Lai** (癩) is the medical term for leprosy, but it is also used colloquially to mean favus of the scalp. For example **laizi** (癩子) is a person affected with favus on the head (Chinese-English dictionary 1979). In her childhood, Beling had a friend with the nickname **Xiao laizi** (小癩子) = the little scabrous, because he often had favus on his head. Colloquially, leprosy is called **mafeng** (麻瘋) (Chinese-English dictionary, 1979). No doubt, leprosy existed at the time of **Zhou**'s visit to Angkor and was considered a dreadful disease. A stone inscription installed by King Yaśovarman I (AD 889-910) setting the rules for the āśrama (ascetic dwelling) in Lolei, mentioned the entry ban for leprous people (Dagens 2005). What **Zhou** saw were most likely the skin diseases such as favus, ringworm, pityriasis, and vitiligo (Figs. 15-01 & 15-02) on people's heads, cheeks, chest, arms and hands that were also common in Cambodia even in the 1940s and 1950s. Ringworm shows rough skin symptoms similar to the early stage of leprosy. The Khmer language has four different words for different types of ringworm diseases. In my childhood, I saw many people with different types of skin diseases. In the 1940s/50s, favus caused by the fungus *Trichophyton schoenleinii*, was common among young children in the Cambodian countryside. Prior to the discovery of the causal fungus by J. L. Schoenlein in 1839, favus was frequently confused with leprosy.

(2) The legend of the Leper King: There are a few versions of the legend of the Leper King - all have their origin in India (Marchal 1955, Porée and Maspéro 1938). In a Hindu scripture (Sāmba Purāna) Sāmba, the grandson of Krishna was afflicted by leprosy (Sahai 2007). Cambodians in different regions know different variations of the legend and most relate it to the statue they call 'Preah Kumlung' = Leprous king, which they think represents King Jayavarman VII. This famous statue in Angkor Thom known to many Khmers as the Leper King is a misnomer; a stone inscription on its pedestal identifies it as Yama, the Hindu

Lord of Death, King of the Underworld. Although the Leper King is a mere legendary figure, some historians tried to speculate about his real existence by interpreting scenes on the bas-reliefs of the Bayon as illustrations of historical facts (Figs. 15-03 & 15-04) [e.g., Coedès 1963; Goloubew in Finot and Goloubew 1930 quoted by Briggs 1951, and Goloubew 1935]. It is hard to believe that any king would allow himself or one of his ancestors to be immortalized in stone as a leprous patient. **Zhou Daguan** himself wrote that it is said (rumoured) that the king had the disease. It was certainly not King Indravarman III who **Zhou** saw during his stay in Angkor, nor King Jayavarman VIII who was the father-in-law of Indravarman III. However, Chandler (1979 and 2000) believed Jayavarman VIII to be the Leper King. The Khmers like to invent rumours, particularly about important personalities such as princes, monks, etc., whom they do not like. Some rumours eventually become folk tales. Jayavarman VIII had a lot of enemies because of his fanatical belief in Śivaism destroying many Buddhist images and inscriptions, thus causing religious strife between Buddhists and Śivaists.

Fig. 15-04. The Tevadas examine the hand of either Preah Thong or a god (Krishna's grandson Sāmba) who is afflicted with leprosy and is ill laying down on the right (Bayon bas-relief) (Photo S. Uk, 2011).

16
DEATH

There is no coffin for a dead person. Only a sort of mat is used, and [the body] is covered with a cloth. At the front of the funeral procession there are flags, drums and music. Popped [unhusked] rice[1] from two trays are also scattered along the route. The body is carried outside the city. At some remote, uninhabited place, people leave the body and wait for the vultures, dogs or other animals to come to feed on [it][2]. If it is finished very quickly, they say that the dead father or mother is blessed and obtained this reward, but if the corpse is not eaten at all or only partially eaten, they think that the father or mother had committed a sin to end this way. Nowadays, there are also people who use cremation. Usually, these are of Chinese descent. When the father or mother dies, they do not wear special mourning garments. The sons only shave their heads, the daughters only cut their hair to the size of a coin on top of their heads to show their mourning and respect. The king has the tower [stupa] as his burial place, but it is not known to me whether the whole body or only the bones are buried.

Fig. 16-01. Poprice in a silver bowl ready for funeral procession in a village in Siem Reap region (Photo credit Intangible Heritage Research Team, APSARA Authority, Cambodia, 2015).

Notes on: 16. Death

(1) **Zhou Daguan** used the expression **chaomi** (炒米) that literally means 'fried raw husked rice'. However in Khmer funeral processions, popped unhusked rice (similar to popcorn) is thrown forwards and backwards, to the left and the right by a female mourner (next of kin) walking in front of the funeral cortège (Figs. 16-01, 16-02, & 16-03).

(2) Archaeological excavations showed that the ancestors of Angkor people buried their dead with opulent grave goods and much ritual (Higham1989). The custom of leaving corpses to wild animals mentioned by **Zhou** is similar to that practiced in Mongolia, a Buddhist country (Dema 2006). **Zhou**'s remark does not seem to agree with archeological evidence that Angkor was one of the world's largest city in the pre-industrial era (e.g. Evans, et al 2013) where uninhabited field would be a rare exception. Could **Zhou** base his record on rumours. However, the practice of giving corpses for animal consumption as a pious gesture must have existed alongside the burial and cremation methods, for in 1860 King Ang Duong advised his courtiers to cut his flesh after his

Woman throwing poprice

Fig. 16-02. Funeral procession in a village in Siem Reap region (Photo credit Intangible Heritage Research Team, APSARA Authority, Cambodia, 2015).

Fig. 16-03. Funeral procession of a high official in Phnom Penh showing a mourning woman spreading poprice (red arrow) (Photo Sophal Sophanit, 2015).

death and offer it to birds, quadrupeds, and 8-legged animals (spiders?) to feed on. After the king's death, the courtiers and members of the royal family ceremoniously carried out the king's wish. Then, the remains of the king's body were buried in a stupa in the royal palace followed by a traditional Buddhist ceremony (Eng Soth 1969). Aschmoneit (2006) commented that it is a pious act to emulate Buddha who, in one of his many lives, gave a piece of his own flesh to a starving tigress.

17

CULTIVATION

In general, three to four harvests a year are possible. This is because all the four seasons are similar to our 5th and 6th months. Also snow and frost are unknown. This place has rain for one half of the year, but none at all for the other half. From the 4th to the 9th month, it rains every day, but only starts in the afternoon. The water level in the freshwater lake [Tonle Sap] can be as high as seven to eight **zhang** [about 23-26m]. Big trees are submerged leaving only the tip of the crown branches. All people living on the banks move to take shelter on the far side of the mountains.

From the 10th month to the 3rd month of the following year, there is not a drop of rain. On the lake [Tonle Sap] one can travel only with small boats. In areas of deep water, the depth is only three or five **chi** [about 1–2m]. At this time, people move back down again. Those who cultivate the land estimate when the rice would ripen and which area the flood would reach, then they sow the seeds accordingly. They do not use oxen to plough the land. Their ploughing tools, sickles and hoes, although having slightly similar appearance to ours, are constructed[1] differently. There is another kind of wild field where rice often grows without being actually sown. With the water sometimes rising up to one **zhang** [about 3m], the rice plant would also grow to the same height. I think this is another rice variety[2].

On fields or in vegetable cultivation, human manure is not used. People find it disgusting and unclean. The Chinese who arrive in this country also do not talk about the use of human manure in China for fear of being despised. Every two or three families dig one pit together and cover it with grass straw. When it is full, they cover it up with earth and dig another one. After having been to the toilet, they always go into a pond to wash themselves. They use the left hand only and reserve the right hand for taking rice. They laugh at the Chinese going to the toilet using paper to wipe themselves and they do not even want them to come into their houses. There are some women in this country who pass water standing up; ridiculous, ridiculous.

Fig. 17-01. Traditional Khmer plough (Photo S. Uk, 2011).

Fig. 17-02. Traditional Khmer sickle (Photo S. Uk, 2006).

Notes on: 17. Cultivation

(1) We translated the Chinese word **zhì** (制) as 'constructed' to mean that the tools are made based on a different design concept. For example the Chinese plough has two handles, the Khmer normally one and is slightly longer (Fig. 17-01); the Chinese sickle has a curved blade at the end of a simple, straight handle, the Khmer one has a curved handle with a long 'tail' pointing backward to pick-up the lodged rice stems at harvest (Fig. 17-02).

(2) Floating paddy. The tip of the stem always grows to stay above water and can reach 5-6m in length.

18
MOUNTAINS AND RIVERS

Entering this country from **Zhenpu**, I have seen mostly flat forests, dense jungles and large tributaries of the Long River[1]. This kind of scenery continues over several hundreds of **li**. Age-old trees with long rattans form dark, misty, hazy canopies filled with sounds of animal and bird songs. When I reached **bangang**[2], I began to see vast fields without a single tree. All are rice and millet[3] as far as my eyes can see. There are hundreds and thousands of wild oxen[4] flocking into the area. There are also bamboo groves extending hundreds of **li** and those bamboos have thorns at each node. The bamboo shoot has a very bitter taste. There are mountains[5] in all the four cardinal directions.

Fig. 18-01. A female Banteng (*Bos javanicus birmanicus*) with characteristic white hair on the lower part of all four legs in Phnom Tamau Zoo (Photo S. Uk, 2006).

Notes on: 18. Mountains and Rivers

(1) **Zhou** meant the Mekong River.

(2) **Ban** (半) = half, **gang** (港) = river arm (branch), or estuary. We think **bangang** here means 'river branch at half-way'. Sailing up the Mekong River at about the halfway point between the sea and Angkor, one sees four waterways. In Khmer this point is known as 'The Four Faces' where the present day Phnom-Penh city is. In the 13th century Phnom-Penh did not exist as a town. There were probably a few houses along the river banks. This is probably what **Zhou** meant.

(3) **Zhou** used two words, **he** (禾) = cereal group (esp. rice) and **shu** (黍) = Broomcorn millet (*Panicum miliaceum)* [A Chinese-EnglishDictionary 1979]. Presently, Cambodia has mainly rice and no millet while the latter is common in China. Sugarcane is common in Cambodia. Assuming that the flora had not changed since **Zhou**'s visit, it is possible that **Zhou**

Fig. 18-02. River Tonle Sap at Kampong Chhnang Town (Photo S. Uk, 2004).

took sugarcane and tall grass as **shu** (黍) since from the ship he could not tell rice plants from sugarcane or tall grass. Furthermore, **Zhou** was travelling up the Mekong and Tonle Sap rivers during the months of June and July when rice, sugarcane and grass look indistinctively green.

(4) **Zhou** mentioned wild oxen. The three types of wild oxen that **Zhou** saw were most likely the gaur (*Bos gaurus*), the banteng (*Bos javanicus birmanicus*) (Fig. 18-01), and the kouprey (*Bos sauveli*). In the 1950s/60s, herds of banteng could regularly be seen grazing in forest clearings in the northeast province of Kratié (reserve of Phnom Prich – Chay Son 2008). The animals must have been so common in the past as to inspire a folk song that has been included in school books to this day:

> Under late afternoon sun
> The banteng and kouprey
> Gather to feed in mountain clearings.
> The young feed among the young,
> The old among the old.
> They feed in the clearings
> On young tender dwarf bamboo.

(5) As one sails across the Tonle Sap Lake to Angkor, one can see small mountains on all sides, in front, on the left and on the right (Fig. 18-02).

19
PRODUCE

There are many strange types of trees in the mountains. Rhinoceros and elephants gather and breed in the area where there are no trees. The varieties of rare birds and strange animals are countless. The high value products are kingfishers' feathers, ivory, rhinoceros horns and yellow wax. The common products are agarwood[1], cardamom, gamboge[2], sticklac[3] and chaulmoogra oil[4]. The kingfisher is fairly difficult to catch. In the forests there are ponds or water reservoirs with fish. The kingfishers fly out of the woods to feed on those fish. The locals use tree leaves to cover their bodies and sit at the water edge. They put a female decoy kingfisher into a cage to attract the male, hold a small net, wait for the male kingfisher to come and trap it. Sometimes they catch three to five birds per day, and some days none at all.

Ivory can be found only by people who live in the remote mountainous areas. When an elephant dies, it yields only two tusks. Thus, the rumour that elephants shed their tusks every year is not true. The tusks that are obtained from speared elephants are considered the best quality. The tusks taken immediately from an elephant that has just died are of lesser quality. Those from elephants that died in the mountains a few years ago are considered as the lowest quality.

The locals collect yellow wax from a type of bee[5] with a very thin waist like an ant that makes nests in decayed trees in the village. Each village can collect up to two to three thousand pieces of honeycomb[6]. Each piece weighs thirty to forty **jin** [about 15-20kg], whereas the small ones weigh no less than eighteen or nineteen **jin** [about 9-10kg].

Rhinoceros horns that are white with patterns are considered of high quality; the black ones are of lower quality.

The agarwood grows in the forest. The locals cut the wood with great difficulty because it is the heart of the tree that they want. The outside white wood part can be eight to nine **cun**[7] [about 26–30cm] thick. Even a small tree has a layer of this white wood no less than four or five **cun** [about 13–17cm] thick.

Fig. 19-01. Hardened resin from the gamboge trees (*Garcinia hanburyi*) that now grow mainly in the forests of the southwest province of Koh Kong bordering Thailand. The resin is extracted by making a spiral incision in the bark and letting the milky sap drip into a bamboo tube. This sap is left to dry in the bamboo tube before it is broken to release the hardened resin. Before the advent of synthetic pigments, it was used in painting as a source of yellow coloring. Nowadays, the resin is used mainly in traditional medicine (Photo Chhann Yam, 2009).

Fig. 19-02. Sections of tree branches with hardened secretion (sticklac) of the scale insect *Laccifer lacca*. Zhou compares these to the mistletoe on mulberry tree. The sticklac is processed by cleaning and heating to give the finished product called shellac (Photo Chhann Yam, 2009).

Cardamom is cultivated in the mountains by the wild men. The gamboge is a kind of tree resin. The locals cut the tree [bark] with a knife the previous year and let the resin drip for one year. They only start to collect [it] the following year.

Sticklac grows among tree branches just like mulberry mistletoe[8], and is rather hard to find. Chaulmoogra oil is extracted from the seeds of a big tree. The fruit look like coconuts and are round[9]. Each fruit has dozens of seeds.

Sometimes there are black pepper[10] plants that grow like climbers; the fruit bundles droop like **lu cao zi**[11] grass seeds; when raw and green, they [the fruit] give a much hotter taste.

Notes on: 19. Produce

(1) Although the Chinese words **jiangzhen** (降真) and **jiangxiang** (降香) mean fragrant rosewood (*Dalbergia odorifera*), this species is not found outside China. What **Zhou** referred to would be the agarwood (*Aquilaria crassna*) (Khmer: "chann krâsna") since he described that the locals had difficulty in getting the heart of the trees. This tree produces distinctive fragrant heartwood as a result of a mould infection. It is highly valued in Southeast Asia and China for its use in traditional medicine. In Cambodia, agarwood is used as incense and as a component in traditional anti-malarial drugs. Pelliot translated it as laka-wood, (*Dalbergia* spp.). We think that neither Pelliot's laka-wood, nor Harris' rosewood is correct, but Smithies' eaglewood (syn. agarwood) is.

(2) **Huahuang** (畫黃) is a yellow gum which corresponds to Pelliot's translation as gamboge that is obtained from the tree (*Garcinia hanburyi*) (Khmer: "chôr rung"). Besides its use in painting and in varnish, gamboge has been used in traditional Khmer medicine to treat colds, bronchitis, and tapeworm (Fig. 19-01).

(3) Sticklac (**zigeng** 紫梗) is a secretion of a scale insect (*Laccifer lacca*) encrusted around branches of trees (Fig. 19-02) such as *Ficus altissima* or *Combretum quadrangulare*. My father grew the sticklac on *Combretum* trees. In rural Cambodia in the 1940s and 50s, sticklac was used as a silk dye. The solidified cake residue was used as sealing wax or glue to fix agricultural implements such as sticking sickle blades to their handles, or gluing metal pieces to the plough mouldboard. The Khmer plough

Fig. 19-03. Chaulmoogra oil producing tree (*Hydnocarpus anthelminthica*) at the entrance to Prasat Ta Prohm; its ripened fruits and seeds (Photo S. Uk, 2006).

is made of a wooden block shaped into a curved mouldboard with a pointed ploughshare capped with a half-cone-shaped metal blade. The rest of the mouldboard is covered with metal chips to protect it from wear and tear (cf. Fig. 17-01, brown mouldboard).

(4) Chaulmoogra oil (**dafengzi you** 大風子油). **Zhou Daguan**'s later description of the tree with fruit that looked like small round coconuts fits the species *Hydnocarpus anthelmintica* known as the common Chaulmoogra tree (Fig. 19-03). However, the true Chaulmoogra tree (*Hydnocarpus kurzii*) which produces more chaulmoogric acid, has much smaller fruit. Both species produce components of chaulmoogric oil that were used to treat leprosy (Kham 2004) before the advent of antibiotics. If fish eat the flesh of the small fruit of *H. kurzii*, the fish meat will become toxic to humans. In contrast, the flesh of *H. anthelmintica* fruit can be eaten by humans without poisoning them.

(5) **Zhou**'s description of the yellow wax collected from bees that look like ants with nests in decaying trees seems to fit the stingless bees of the genus *Trigona* (Khmer: "pruët"). They produce yellow waxy honeycombs (more wax than liquid honey) in layers about 2cm thick. However, **Zhou**'s weight of the honeycombs is not in agreement with those of the stingless bees that measure 10–15cm in diameter and weigh no more than one kg. **Zhou**'s description of big honeycombs weighing 15kg or more however, fits those of the giant honeybee (*Apis dorsata*) which build massive single honeycombs of 1.5 x 1m. However, the giant honeybees build nests of large single honeycombs on big tree branches in open spaces high above the ground (Fig. 19-04). There are at least two other species of wild honeybees, the dwarf honeybee (*Apis florea*) and the black dwarf honeybee (*Apis andreniformis*). These species build single honeycomb nests around small tree branches, each honeycomb measuring about 10 x 15cm (Oldroyd and Wongsiri 2006). **Zhou** must have gathered the information on beeswax collection from different local Chinese residents and lumped together different types of bees into one type that looked unusual to him. So he described only the stingless bee that is different from the normal honeybee.

(6) The original text says 'each boat'. **Jin Ronghua** thought that the word 'boat' could be an error since there is no mention of any location near waterways. Furthermore, an ordinary Khmer boat cannot carry two to three thousand pieces of honeycomb each weighing at least 18 **jin** (9kg). This would mean one river boat carrying at least 18 tons of honeycombs – impossible.

Fig. 19-04. Giant wild honeybee's nest on branches of *Tetrameles nudiflora* whose roots grip the walls of Prasat Ta Prohm and Prasat Preah Khan (Photo S. Uk, 2013).

(7) **Cun** = 0.1 **chi** = about 3.3cm.

(8) **Zhou** compares the sticklac to **sang jisheng** (桑寄生) which is a shrub-like evergreen parasitic plant (*Loranthus parasiticus*) found mostly on mulberry and persimmon trees, and known as mulberry mistletoe (Chinese Language Dictionary - **Xinhua Hanyu Cidian** 2007). Sticklac is a scarlet colored resinous secretion of a scale insect (*Laccifer lacca*). On contact with air it hardens and, where the insects are closely crowded together, it forms a continuous crusty layer over small branches of certain trees (usually *Combretum quadrangulare*). From a distance, it looks somewhat like mistletoe (cf. Fig. 19-02).

(9) See note (4).

(10) Black pepper vine, *Piper nigrum*.

(11) **Lu cao zi** (綠草子) literally means 'green grass seeds'.

20
TRADE

In this country, buying and selling can be done by all women. This is the reason why a Chinese man who arrives here must first find himself a woman so as to obtain extra benefit from her trading skills. Every day, there is a market from dawn until mid-day. There are no shops that people can live in[1]. They just lay something like a mat on the ground; each has her own usual place. I have heard that people pay rent for the ground space to the officials. In small tradings, they pay with rice and Chinese goods. Next step up they pay with copper coins[2]. For the big businesses, the payment is with gold and silver.

Generally speaking, the natives are very simple and down-to-earth. When they meet a Chinese, they are respectful and afraid. They call the Chinese 'Buddha' and they prostrate themselves in greeting. Recently, due to many new arrivals there has been some cheating and bullying of the Chinese.

Notes on: 20. Trade

(1) From **Zhou**'s point of view, daily trading activities would normally be carried out in a shop that also serves as living quarters (Fig. 20-01).

(2) See note (3) in Chapter 9 ' Slaves'.

Fig. 20-01. Khmer market women weighing goods while two Chinese residents pass comments as noted by Freeman & Jacques (2006) (Photo S. Uk, 2006).

21
DESIRABLE CHINESE GOODS

This country probably does not produce gold or silver. Chinese gold and silver are the number one preferences, then come the colorful, thin, fine silk fabrics[1]. Next are the pewter ware from **Zhenzhou**[2], lacquered trays[3] from **Wenzhou**, celadon ware from **Quanzhou**[4], and mercury, vermillion, paper, sulphur, saltpetre, sandalwood[5], angelica, musk, linen, **huangcao bu**[6], umbrellas, iron woks or pots, copper trays, crystal [or porcelain] beads, tung oil, fine-tooth combs[7], wood combs and needles. The bulky and heavy goods, for example, mats from **Mingzhou**[8] are also in demand. The really desirable goods are beans and wheat, but they cannot be exported [out of China][9].

Fig. 21-01. Reproduction of ancient Chinese fine-tooth comb, bizi (篦子), for combing hair and lice; is usually double-sided as this modern reproduction. We both used it in our childhood in our separate villages [Solang in Touk Meas, Cambodia, Beling in Hunan, China] (Photo S. Uk, 2006).

Notes on: 21. Desirable Chinese goods

(1) **Jianbo** (縑帛) = fine thin silk fabrics that can be used for writing on like paper.

(2) **Zhenzhou** (真州) in the **Yuan** dynasty is today's **Yizheng** (儀徵) County in **Jiangsu** Province.

(3) **Pan** (盤) = any shallow plate, dish, saucer, tray, etc..

(4) Celadon is a porcelain produced in the city of **Quanzhou** (泉州) in **Fujian** Province. The town of **Chuzhou** (處州) in **Zhejiang** Province with its famous **Longquan** (龍泉) kiln also produces celadon. This latter town is also mentioned in another version of **Zhou**'s Record (**Jin Ronghua** 1976).

(5) Scientific name *Santalum album*.

(6) **Huangcao bu** (黃草布) literally means 'yellow straw fabric'. According to **Jin Ronghua**, it is a fabric made in **Gui'an** county in the **Zhejiang** Province.

(7) **Bizi** (篦子) is a fine-tooth comb usually (but not always) double-sided, for combing hair or especially for combing out lice and nits [Khmer: "snët"] (Fig. 21-01). We both used it in our childhood in our separate villages [Solang in Touk Meas, Cambodia, **Beling** in **Hunan**, China]. Elderly people like to use it to massage their heads. **Zhou** wrote it down as **biji** (篦箕). Harris (quoted **Xia Nai**) thought it could be a dialect word from **Zhou**'s home town **Wenzhou**, but the Chinese language dictionary (**Xinhua Hanyu Cidian** 2007) mentions that **bizi** and **biji** can be used interchangeably to mean fine-tooth comb. Currently, it is known as **bizi** in **Hunan**, **Hubei**, and **Sichuan** Provinces.

(8) **Mingzhou** (明州) is today's **Ningbo**, south of **Shanghai**.

(9) In the **Yuan** dynasty, the export of all cereal products was forbidden.

22

PLANTS AND TREES

There are pomegranates, sugarcane, lotus flowers, lotus roots, carambolas[1], bananas, and **xiongqiong**[2] as in China. Although lychees and tangerines are the same in shape as the Chinese ones, they taste sour. There are many other kinds [of fruit] I have never seen in China. Trees are also very different. There are so many varieties of herbaceous plants and flowers. The flowers are scented and with beautiful vibrant colors. There are even more varieties of flowers in the water, but I do not know their names. As for peaches, plums, apricots, sour plums, pines, cypresses, firs, Chinese junipers, pears, Chinese dates[3], poplars, willows, osmanthus[4], orchids, chrysanthemums[5] - this country does not have them. However, there are lotus flowers in the first lunar month[6].

Fig. 22-01. The carambola (star fruit) tree with its ripening fruits (Photo S. Uk, 1999).

Notes on: 22. Plants and Trees

(1) The original text was **yu tao** (芋桃) meaning 'taro peach' which does not exist. **Jin Ronghua** and **Xia Nai** independently changed it to **yangtao** (羊桃). This is the common name for carambola or star fruit (*Averrhoa carambola*) (Chinese-English Dictionary 1979, and New Age English-Chinese Dictionary 2004), but the Chinese Dictionary from the P.R.C. (Chinese Language Dictionary - **Xinhua Hanyu Cidian** 2007) gives the alternative meaning of **yangtao** as **mihoutao** (猕猴桃), the Chinese gooseberry or Kiwi fruit (*Actinidia deliciosa*). Since the Chinese gooseberry is a temperate plant that does not grow in Cambodia, **yangtao** must mean carambola which is a tropical fruit plant (**Xia Nai** 2000). Pelliot also translated as carambola (Fig. 22-01).

(2) The original text **xiong** (芎) is actually **xiongqiong** (芎藭), also known as **chuanxiong** (川芎) or **Szechuan** lovage (*Ligusticum wallichii* or *L. chuanxiong*). It is a flowering plant of the carrot family whose roots are used in Chinese medicine. This plant does not exist in Cambodia. Maybe **Zhou** talked about another plant that looked similar to **Szechuan** lovage.

(3) Chinese dates or Jujube = *Ziziphus zizyphus*.

(4) The word **gui** (桂) can mean cinnamon or osmanthus. The latter has fragrant flowers that give a special meaning to the Chinese. Osmanthus must have been what **Zhou** meant; Cambodia has cinnamon but does not have osmanthus.

(5) After the word 'chrysanthemums' there is a word '**rui**' (蕊) which means 'flower heart', i.e., pistil or stamen. This makes no sense. **Jin Ronghua** thought it could be a script error and changed the word to **zhi** (芷) since the latter can be a plant with white flowers, e.g., **baizhi** (白芷) (*Dahurian angelica*) whose roots are used in traditional Chinese medicine

(6) This sentence about the lotus flowers is odd since they were mentioned at the beginning of the chapter. Maybe **Zhou** wrote it as an explanatory note to inform Chinese readers that the lotus in Cambodia flowers all year round, even during the Chinese winter months (**Jin Ronghua** 1976).

23
FLYING BIRDS

Among the birds here, there are peacocks, kingfishers and parrots that do not exist in China. There are other birds such as vultures, crows, cormorants, sparrows, storks[1], cranes, wild ducks and siskins[2] that we also have in China. In this country there are no magpies, wild swans[3], orioles, cuckoos[4], swallows or pigeons.

Fig. 23-01. The Grey Heron (*Ardea cinerea*) in a zoo near Angkor Park (Photo S. Uk, 2006).

Notes on: 23. Flying Birds

(1) The original word **guan** (鸛) = stork. Storks in Chinese mean the group of large, long-legged, long-necked wading birds including the 'true' storks of the family Ciconiidae and the heron group of the family Ardeidae (there are a few long-legged Ardeidae species in Cambodia). Pelliot's translation as cigogne (the European stork) is not quite correct since this stork does not exist in Cambodia. However other storks, such as the Grey Heron (*Ardea cinerea*) (Fig. 23-01) and the Lesser Adjutant (*Leptoptilos javanicus*) (Fig. 23-02) are common in Cambodia (Davidson 2009).

(2) Pelliot: canaries with a question mark.

(3) Pelliot: wild geese

(4) Pelliot: nightjars.

Fig. 23-02. The Lesser Adjutant (*Leptoptilos javanicus*) in Tamau Zoo (Photo S. Uk, 2005).

24
WALKING ANIMALS

Their animals such as rhinoceroses, elephants, wild oxen[1] and mountain horses[2] are those that China does not have. The others such as tigers, panthers, bears, wild boar, milu (Père David's deer), deer, river deer, muntjac, apes and foxes exist in abundance. What they lack are lions, **xingxing** [chimpanzees][3] and camels. Of course there are chickens, ducks, oxen [buffaloes], horses, pigs and goats here also. The horses are very small, and there are a lot of cattle also. When the cattle are alive, people dare not ride on them and when they are dead people dare not eat their meat or take their skin. They just let them rot away because the live cattle have helped people to do work. They use them to pull the oxcart. Earlier there were no geese, but recently the boat people brought the geese in from China; so there are some here now. Some rats are as big as cats. There is also one kind of rat with the head exactly resembling that of a newborn puppy.

Notes on: 24. Walking Animals

(1) Wild oxen are most likely the banteng (*Bos javanicus birmanicus*) and/or the related species, kouprey (*Bos sauveli*). The latter is a critically endangered species, possibly now extinct.

(2) There is no record of wild or mountain horses in Cambodia. Was **Zhou** confused with the female deer when seen from the distance?

(3) **Xingxing** (猩猩) is a group of large apes without tails that includes the orang outan (this does not exist in China), the gorilla (big **xingxing**, also does not exist in China) and the chimpanzee (black **xingxing**). Chimpanzee is most likely what **Zhou Daguan** meant.

Fig. 24-01. A bear in Phnom Tamau open zoo. Deforestation threatens many wildlife that may now be only found in the zoo (Photo S. Uk, 2005).

25
VEGETABLES

As vegetables, there are green onion, mustard, Chinese leek, aubergine, gourd, water melon, wax gourd, cucumber and amaranthus[1]. Vegetables such as white radish, lettuce, endive, and spinach are not available here. Aubergine, gourd, cucumber and wax gourd are available from the first lunar month onwards. Some aubergine plants can grow for many years without being pulled out. Kapok trees[2] can be taller than the houses, some stand more than 10 years without being replaced. There are many other types of vegetables that I do not know the names of, and there are also many kinds that grow in water.

Notes on: 25. Vegetables

(1) Amaranthus: Chinese **xian cai** (莧菜), also known as Chinese spinach, (Khmer: "phti") is a very popular vegetable in China and Southeast Asia. It belongs to the group *Amaranthus* spp. This is what **Zhou** referred to, and not the ornamental flowering species or the grain producing species such as *Amaranthus hybridus* and *Amaranthus tricolor*.

(2) Kapok trees that can grow to 10m high are more pertinent to **Zhou**'s description (Fig. 11-01). Pelliot's translation as cotton trees is not quite correct since it can be confused with the tree cotton (*Gossypium arboreum*) that grows to only 2m in height.

26
FISH AND DRAGONS

Of fish and turtles[1], the black carp are the most abundant. Other fish such as the common carp, crucian carp and grass carp are also in abundance. Big goby[2] fish [marble goby] weigh more than two **jin** [>1 kg]. There are many fish types for which I do not know the names. All the above fish are from the Fresh Water Lake [Tonle Sap Lake]. As for salt water fish, there are also many kinds. The natives do not eat finless eels and white eels[3] or frogs[4]; thus at night one can see frogs jumping across the road.

Soft-shelled turtles and monitor lizards[5] are as big as **hezhu**[6]. People here even eat land tortoises[7]. The prawns[8] in **Zhanan** [Kampong Chhnang] weigh more than one **jin** [0.5kg]. The goose barnacles[9] from **Zhenpu** can be more than eight or nine **cun** [about 26–30cm] long.

The big crocodiles can be the size of a boat, have four legs, and are very similar to dragons but without horns. Their stomachs[10] are very crunchy and taste delicious. Clams, cockles, snails, etc. can be obtained by just cupping one's hands into the Fresh Water Lake [Tonle Sap Lake]. Only crabs have not been seen. I think there are also crabs here, but people do not eat them.

Fig. 26-01. The marble goby (*Oxyeleotris marmorata*) is similar to the much smaller Chinese tubu (*Odontobutis obscura*) (Photo Nirano Tek, 2009).

Fig. 26-02. The monitor lizard (in a zoo near Angkor Park) is hunted in the wild for its delicious meat; its skin is used in drum making (Photo S. Uk, 2006).

Fig. 26-03. Soft shell turtle in a zoo near Angkor Park (Photo S. Uk, 2006).

Notes on: 26. Fish and Dragons

(1) The text in **Wu Guan**'s edition is **yu long** (魚龍) which means 'Fish and Dragons", but in **Shuo fu**'s edition the text is **yu bie** (魚鱉) = 'Fish and Soft-shelled Turtle'. The word 'dragons' in the **Wu Guan**'s edition must refer to the monitor lizards which **Zhou** mentioned later in the chapter - see note (5).

(2) **Tubu** (吐哺), also known as **tufu** (土附) is a bottom dweller goby species (*Odontobutis obscura*) of the family Eleotridae (**Zhang Chunguang** 2007). It is a relatively small fish (max. length 12cm) and is highly prized in Chinese cuisine in the **Ningbo** area, **Zhejiang** Province where **Zhou Daguan** came from. In Cambodia there is a similar fish of the same family, the marble goby (*Oxyeleotris marmorata*). It is commercially fished when it reaches an average length of 30cm. However it can grow to 50-60cm and weigh several kg (Fig. 26-01). This probably caught **Zhou**'s attention because it looks like the **tubu** in China, but is much bigger. Presently Cambodia exports (by air freight) live marble goby to Hong Kong and Taiwan.

(3) Swamp eel (*Monopterus albus*). White eel, unidentified.

(4) It was known in the 1950s that people in Siem Reap (Angkor area) did not eat eels and frogs.

(5) In the Chinese dictionary, **tuolong** (鼉龍) is a kind of alligator commonly known as 'pig-cheek dragon' whose skin can be used in drum-making. This fits the description of the monitor lizards (Fig. 26-02). Pelliot queried his own translation as 'alligator'.

(6) **Hezhu** (合苧) does not have any logical meaning in Chinese (**Jin Ronghua**, and **Xia Nai**). Pelliot did not translate it and it does not seem to be a transliteration of Khmer either.

(7) According to **Jin Ronghua**, the other name for tortoise is **zang liu** (藏六) meaning 'to hide the six parts' - the four feet, plus the head and the tail (making up the six parts) that can be retracted into the shell. In times gone by, Chinese people would eat the soft-shelled turtle, but never the hard-shelled land tortoise; the shell of the latter is used as an oracle. Pelliot questioned his own translation as 'turtle of six **tsang**' (Fig. 26-03).

(8) The giant river prawn (*Macrobrachium rosenbergii*).

(9) The Chinese word **guijiao** (龜脚) [or **guizu** (龜足) in the Chinese dictionary] literally means 'turtle's foot'; it is the goose barnacles that live attached to rocks and looks like a turtle's foot.

(10) The word in **Wu Guan**'s edition is **du** (肚) meaning 'stomach'. **Xia Nai** following **Shuo fu**'s edition, changed the text to **cheng** (蟶) which means razor clam. **Jin Ronghua** kept the text as **du** (stomach) and Pelliot also translated it as [crocodile] stomach since the word logically refers to crocodile. Razor clams are marine animals whereas the Khmer crocodiles live in fresh water. **Zhou** described clams, cockles and snails as being easy to gather by just scooping them up with hands in Tonle Sap Lake and he did not mention taste. Thus to lump the text 'razor clams are very crunchy and taste delicious' with the latter group seems out of context.

27
FERMENTING ALCOHOL

There are four grades of alcoholic drink in this country; the first grade is called honey wine by the Chinese and is fermented by adding yeast to a half-half mixture of honey and water. The next grade, which the locals call **pengyasi**, is made from **pengyasi**[1] leaves, a type of tree. The next, made from fermented raw rice or left-over cooked rice, is called **bao lengjiao** because **bao lengjiao**[2] means raw rice. The grade further down is called sugar wine which is made from sugar. Additionally, when one goes into the river tributaries, one encounters another type of alcoholic drink called 'jiao juice wine' which is a wine made from leaves of **jiao**[3] grass which grows along the river banks; its juice can be used for wine fermentation.

Notes on: 27. Fermenting Alcohol

(1) Pelliot: **pengyasi** (朋牙四) is not positively identified but Pelliot suggested a small tree (2-5m high) called "ph'ngiës" (*Memocylon* spp.). This tree is not known to be used in fermenting drinks, but it has been used in traditional Khmer medicine.

(2) **Bao** (包) must be the transliteration of Khmer "bai" = cooked rice, and **lengjiao** (棱角), the old Khmer "rongkor" = raw husked rice. Writing his record back in China after his return from Cambodia, **Zhou**'s memory of some Khmer words might have been somewhat blurred.

(3) The word **jiao** (茭) is most likely the transliteration of the Khmer word "chāk" which means the nipa palm (*Nypa fruticans*). This is a stemless palm that grows in brackish rivers near the sea. Its leaves are used for wrapping cakes or for roofing. The juice exuded from its tapped inflorescence can be fermented into alcohol (Fig. 27-01). In mentioning juice from leaves, **Zhou** probably made an erroneous guess for the same reason in (2) above.

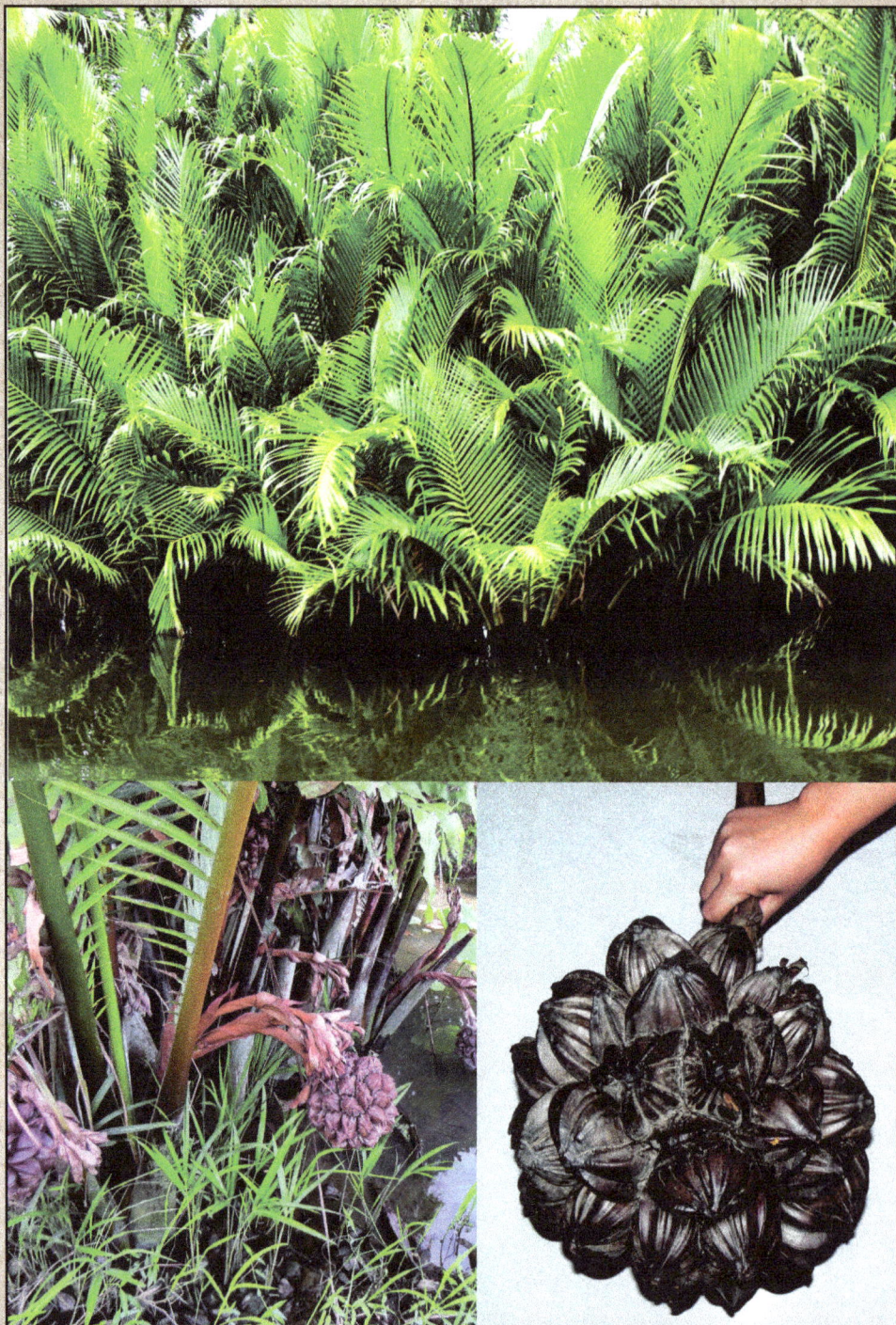

Fig. 27-01. Nipa palm (*Nypa fruticans*) and fruit cluster. Its leaves are used for wrapping rice cakes and for roofing. The juice from specially cut flowers can be fermented into alcohol (Photo Nirano Tek, 2006).

28
SALT, VINEGAR, SOY PASTE AND QU

Salt can be produced in this country without restrictions. Along the coast from **Zhenpu**[1] and **Bajian**[2] and other places people produce salt from heating sea water. In the mountains there is a kind of stone that tastes better than salt and can be carved into objects. The natives do not know how to make vinegar. If they like to have soup sour, they put tamarind[3] leaves into it. If the tree bears pods[4], then they use the pods. If the tree bears seeds [mature fruit], then they use the seeds[5]. People do not know how to make soy sauce because there are no wheat or soya beans. They also do not make **qu**[6]. To make alcoholic drinks they use honey, water and plant leaves for fermentation. The wine yeast[7] they use is similar to the white wine yeast in our villages.

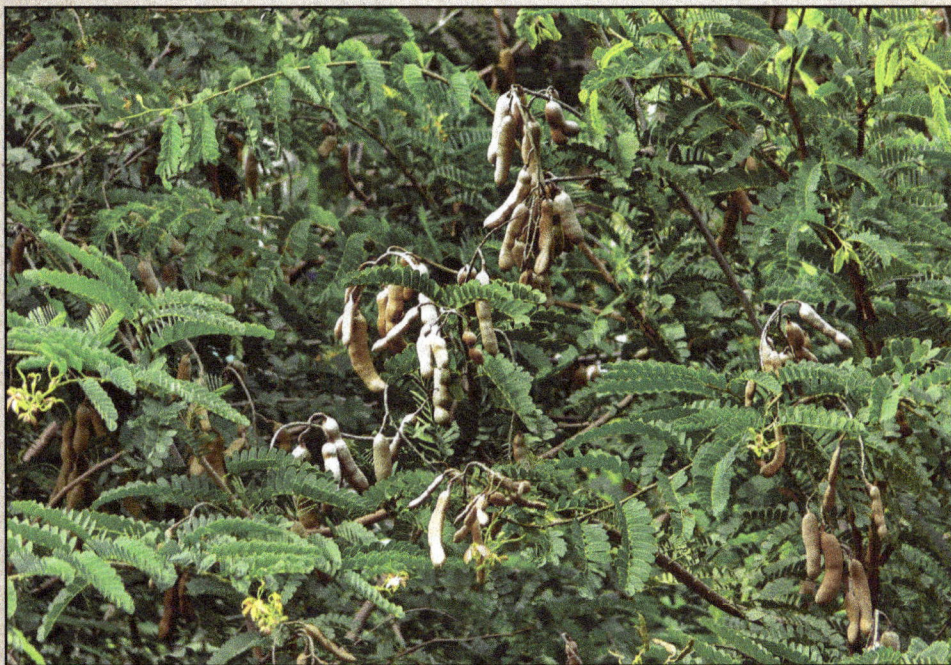

Fig. 28-01. Tamarind tree with fruits (Photo S. Uk, 2004).

Notes on: 28. Salt, Vinegar, Soy Paste and Qu

(1) **Zhenpu** (真蒲) is present day Baria in South Vietnam (Khmer: "Preah Suorkier").

(2) **Bajian** (巴㵎) is possibly present day **Ba Xuyên** (formerly Sôc Trang) in South Vietnam. (Khmer: "Khleang" or "Bassac").

(3) The Chinese word **xianping** (咸平) is the transliteration of the Khmer word "âmpoel" = tamarind (*Tamarindus indica*).

(4) **Zhou Daguan** used the word **jia** (荚) which is the botanical name for the fruits of the bean family of plants. Tamarind is in the bean family; young leaves or fruit (green or ripe) are used as source of tartness in soups and in sauces.

(5) People use the flesh around the seeds of the ripened fruits.

(6) In China a piece of **qu** (麴) is used for starting the fermentation. This '**qu**' is made from yeast mixed with either barley, soya or bran. It is normally sold in the market as white balls the size of cherries for home use.

(7) The Chinese text is **Jiuyao** (酒藥) = wine yeast.

29

SILKWORMS AND MULBERRY TREES

The natives do not rear silkworms or grow mulberry trees. Women do not know needlework, sewing or darning. They only know how to weave the kapok cloth, but do not know how to spin yarn using a spinning wheel. They just make threads with their fingers. They have no loom, but wind the [cloth] head to their waist and weave the other end[1]. A bamboo tube is used as shuttle. In recent years some Siamese came here to settle. They planted mulberry trees and raised silkworms. All the mulberry and silk worm varieties were brought in from Siam. This country has no **mazhu**, only **luoma**[2]. The Siamese women can weave thin silk themselves for clothing. They can sew and darn. If the natives' clothes are torn, they ask the Siamese women to mend for them.

Notes on: 29. Silkworms and Mulberry Trees

(1) The word **dā** (搭) can mean to put up, to connect, to come into contact with, to put over or to hang over. Both **Jin Ronghua** and **Xia Nai** added the word 'window' after **dā** to give the meaning of the text as 'hanging over the window'. Such a sentence does not fit the practical view point – how can one continue weaving when the yarns are on the other side of the window. Furthermore, the windows of the traditional Khmer houses do not lend themselves to such a work (cf. Fig. 09-01) because the insides of the houses are dark. Maybe the text has been corrupted.

(2) We do not translate **mazhu** and **luoma** for the following reasons:

- **Mazhu** (麻苧) could be the inversion of **zhuma** (苧麻) which means ramie or China grass (*Boehmeria nivea*). Ramie is commonly grown in tropical Asia including Cambodia.

- **Luoma** (絡麻) could be the **Wenzhou** dialect for **dama** (大麻) (**Xia Nai** 2000) which means hemp (*Cannabis sativa*). The tall fiber producing hemp was not common in Cambodia in the 1940s and 50s.

Even if **Zhou** meant ramie and hemp, the mention of these two plants seems out of context in a chapter on silkworms and mulberry trees.

30
Utensils

The ordinary people have houses but do not have tables, stools, bowls, buckets, etc. They use clay cauldrons[1] to cook rice and baked clay pots[2] to cook soup. They bury three stones in the ground to form a fire stove. They use coconut shells as ladles and use Chinese clay plates or copper plates to serve rice. As for soup, they put it in small bowls made of tree leaves. These small bowls can hold liquid sauce without leaking. They also use a **jiao**[3] leaf to make a small spoon to take sauce or liquid to the mouth. After use, they throw it away. Even food offerings to gods and Buddha are served in the same manner. They put water in a tin or a clay vessel nearby for rinsing their hands. They use only their hands to take rice. This sticks to them. Without this water it will not come off. For drinking wine, they

Fig. 30-01. Parading soldiers with family pause to cook; one man kneels to blow fire under a pot, other two sit around a tall pot (Bayon bas-relief) (Photo S. Uk, 2011).

use pewter[4] wine pots. Poor people use clay bowls, but the officials and [people of] the rich houses use silverware or even goldware. For national celebrations, most of the utensils are of gold; the dimensions and shapes are also different.

On the floor, they lay straw mats from **Mingzhou**, or skins of tiger, panther, muntjac or deer, etc., or rattan mats. Currently, they use low tables of just over one **chi** [about 30cm] in height. For sleeping, they only use bamboo mats[5] on wooden boards. Recently, some also use low beds, generally all made by Chinese.

They cover food with cloth[6]. In the royal palace they use fine thin silk with melted gold specks which are all gifts from foreign merchants. To polish rice they do not use a grinding mill, but a pestle and mortar instead.

Notes on: 30. Utensils

(1) **Fu** (釜) = cauldron. In the past, the Khmers used baked clay cauldrons for cooking rice (Fig. 30-01).

(2) **Diao** (銚) = baked clay pot with a round handle on one side and a pouring lip on the side at 90° to the handle. In the 1940s, my mother used to use a sort of **diao** for frying.

(3) Possibly the leaves of nipa palm (*Nypa fruticans*), or **Zhou** could have mistaken the leaves of the Khmer sugar palm that grow around people's houses.

(4) **La** (鑞) = pewter. However, pewter utensils have not been found by archeologists in the Angkor area.

(5) Traditional mats in Cambodia are made from reeds or rushes (*Cyperus elatus* or *C. cyperoides*). These mats look very much like they are made from finely polished bamboo strips. Cambodian bamboos are normally split into strips of about 2-cm wide to make coarse mats which are used as walls in thatch huts. They are very uncomfortable to sleep on.

(6) **Jin Ronghua** and **Xia Nai** following the **Shuo fu** edition, used the text containing 'There are a lot of mosquitoes. At night they also cover themselves with cloth-nets'. However in the **Wu Guan** edition, the text says: 'They cover food with cloths'. We think that the latter is more relevant based on the fact that in the 1940s-1960s, mosquito nets were a luxury item affordable only by the well-off people in the cities. In the countryside, despite mosquitoes and endemic malaria, poor people could not afford mosquito nets. Near to the houses, people in villages resorted to making permanent fires with big piles of rice or coconut husks. This produced a large amount of smoke in order to keep mosquitoes away from people as well as from cattle and buffaloes.

On the other hand, at family or religious ceremonies, it is a common practice to cover trays of food to protect them from flies. There is a special gadget called "sachi" made for the purpose. It is a cone-shaped bamboo frame with a base diameter of 30-50cm with a net of fine cloth sewn around it. Rich families use thin, transparent fabric with golden specks similar to **Zhou**'s description.

31
CARTS AND PALANQUINS

In making a palanquin, people take a piece of wood that is bent in the middle with both ends [curved] upwards. It is carved with patterns and strapped with silver or gold foils. This is the so-called gold- or silver-handled palanquin. Hooks are fixed about one **chi** [about 30cm] from each end of the handle. A large piece of folded heavy cloth is tied with ropes to these hooks. A person crouches in this cloth piece and is carried by two men[1,2]. Besides the palanquin, there is an additional thing in the shape of a sampan roof-cover but broader and decorated with colorful silk cloth. It is carried by four men escorting the palanquin. For long distance trips, some ride on elephants and horses as well as carts. The carts in this country are made the same way as those in other countries. However, the horses[3] have no saddles whereas on the elephants there are benches[4] to sit on.

Notes on: 31. Carts and Palanquins

(1) See Fig. 31-01. A queen riding royal palanquin.

(2) See Fig. 31-02. A person riding a palanquin for ordinary people.

(3) See Fig. 31-03. An officer riding horse without saddle.

(4) The original text says 'there are no benches', but **Jin Ronghua** argued that the sculptures on the Bayon bas-reliefs and elsewhere always show elephants with benches (howdah without canopy) on their backs (Fig. 31-04); so he changed his version of the text to 'there are benches'.

Fig. 31-01. A queen riding royal palanquin with carved ends strapped with gold leaf. Angkor Wat South Gallery (Photo Kent Davis).

Fig. 31-02. A person riding a palanquin for ordinary people (Bayon bas-relief) (Photo S. Uk, 2011).

Fig. 31-03. An officer riding a horse without a saddle as mentioned by Zhou Daguan (Bayon bas-relief) (Photo S. Uk, 2001).

Fig. 31-04. Officers sitting on benches (howdah) on elephants' backs (Bayon bas-relief) (Photo S. Uk, 2001).

32
BOATS AND OARS

Large boats are made by assembling planks split from hard wood. The workers have no saws. They use adzes to split the wood into planks. This wastes both wood and time. Every time they want to cut timber into sections, they use chisels to chisel through the wood. Even in house building, they still use the same method.

In building big boats, they also use iron nails. To cover them, they use **jiao**[1] leaves pressed down by strips of areca wood[2]. This kind of boat is called **xinna**[3]. They also use oars. They seal and oil the boat using fish oil mixed with lime.

Small boats are made by hollowing out a big tree trunk to form a trough, then they use fire to smoke and soften it in order to insert wood pieces to expand the center. This boat is big-bellied with both ends pointed. There is no canopy; it can carry several persons. It is rowed only with paddles and is called a **pilan**[4].

Fig. 32-01. Boats rowed by several oarsmen described by Zhou as Pilan (Bayon bas-relief) (Photo S. Uk, 2006).

Fig. 32-02. Oarsmen preparing for the race on Tonle Sap River in front of the Royal Palace during the Water Festival in November. Most boats are still made in the same way as described by Zhou (Photo Nirao Tek, 2010).

Fig. 32-03. Dugouts are still being made in Cambodia using the technique described by Zhou Daguan. The tree is hollowed out and then placed on embers so that the walls of the boat can be expanded with the heat. The photograph from 2008 shows an unfinished dugout that has been abandoned in the precinct of a pagoda in Chong Khneas (Photo V. Walker Vadillo, 2008).

Notes on: 32. Boats and Oars

(1) **Jiao** (茭) (Khmer: "chāk") = nipa palm (*Nypa fruticans*). The leaves are still used for roofing in areas where the plant grows. In other areas of Cambodia, leaves of the sugar or coconut palm are widely used.

(2) Most likely the areca palm (*Areca catechu*). It is commonly grown around houses. Its fruit is used in betel nut chewing. Aged trees are cut down and their trunks split and used in hut construction when strength and durability are not critical, or for purposes as described by **Zhou**.

(3) **Xinna** (新拏): Pelliot could not determine the origin of the word and suggested something like "senda". Ly Thiam Teng suggested "sândâr", a type of medium-size boat still common in present day Cambodia.

(4) On the bas-relief of Bayon there are scuptures of small, narrow boats with several oarsmen (Fig. 32-01). **Zhou**'s description of how a **pilan** (皮闌) was made fits the modern making of the racing pirogue (Khmer: "toūk prânaing" or "toūk ngôr") used during the Water Festival in November (Fig. 32-02). It is made in a Buddhist pagoda from a dugout trunk of *Hopea odorata* ritually selected by monks (Chhann Yam, personal communication 2009, Hoc Cheng Siny 2001, and Waker Vadillo 2015) (Fig. 32-03). The word "prânaing" is commonly pronounced "p'naing" (the r sound is swallowed up and cannot be heard). This could be transliterated into Chinese as **pilan** since the Chinese often cannot distinguish the sound of N and L and lacks a clear sound ng/ŋ at the end.

33
PROVINCES

There are more than 90 provinces named: **Zhenpu**[1], **Zhanan**[2], **Bajian**[3], **Moliang**[4], **Baxue**[5], **Pumai**[6], **Zhigun**[7], **Mujinbo**[8], **Laigankeng**[9], **Basili**[10]. The rest, I cannot recall. Each province has its officials and cities have wooden palisades.

Fig. 33-01. Zhou's Zhanan is the town of Kampong Chhnang. The province of the same name is well known for its pottery production (Photo S. Uk, 2005).

Notes on: 33. Provinces

(1) Present day Baria-Vung Tau near to Saigon in South Vietnam.

(2) Present day Kampong Chhnang Province, north of Phnom-Penh famous for potery making (Fig. 33-01).

(3) **Bajian** (巴墹) is possibly present day Ba Xuyên (formerly Sôc Trang) in South Vietnam. (Khmer: "Khleang" or "Bassac").

(4) **Molieng** or Malyang, an area southeast of Battambang and north of Pôsat (Pursat). The people had the same name as the province, but they now seem to be extinct. The name was found on stone inscriptions K.451 and Ka 64 (Coedès 1968 and Vong 2003).

(5) Possibly Paksè, in present day Laos (Smithies 2001, Harris 2007).

(6) Most likely Phimai, in present day Thailand (Smithies 2001, Harris 2007).

(7) Possibly the present day district of Skuôn, in the western part of Kampong Cham Province, northeast of Phnom-Penh on the road to Angkor. Saigon has been suggested, but this should be rejected on the basis that the area around Saigon would be part of the province of **Zhenpu** mentioned many times by **Zhou** (13th century), and Saigon is the 19th century Vietnamese name of the Khmer town of Prey Nokor.

(8) Unidentified.

(9) Unidentified.

(10) Possibly Possilan (Briggs 1951), in the present day Chantaburi Province of Thailand.

34
VILLAGES

Each village has a pagoda or a tower[1]. If the population density is a little higher, the village has its own managing official called **mai jie**[2]. On main roads, there are resting places similar to our postal pavilions called **senmu**[3]. But recently due to the war with the Siamese, those places have been turned into waste land.

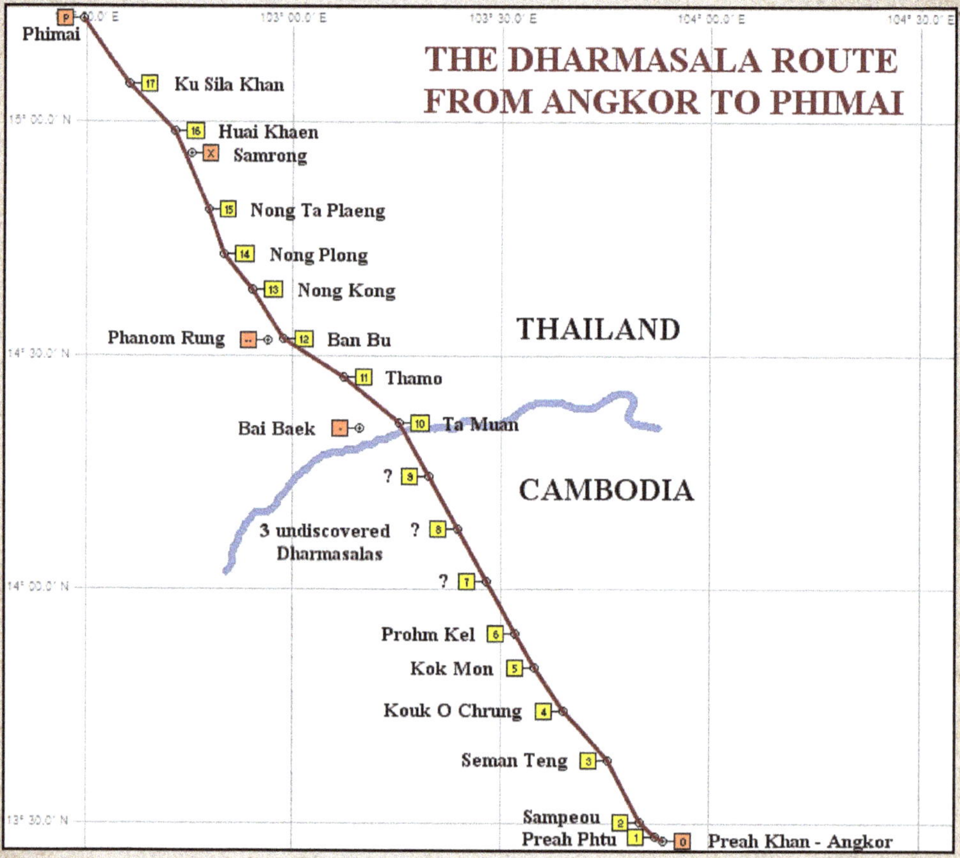

THE DHARMASALA ROUTE FROM ANGKOR TO PHIMAI

Phimai

Ku Sila Khan — 17

Huai Khaen — 16
Samrong — X

Nong Ta Plaeng — 15

Nong Plong — 14

Nong Kong — 13

Phanom Rung — Ban Bu — 12

Thamo — 11

Bai Baek — Ta Muan — 10

? — 9

3 undiscovered Dharmasalas   ? — 8

? — 7

Prohm Kel — 6

Kok Mon — 5

Kouk O Chrung — 4

Seman Teng — 3

Sampeou — 2
Preah Phtu — 1 — 0 — Preah Khan - Angkor

THAILAND

CAMBODIA

Fig. 34-01. Map of ancient highway showing location of Dharmasalars (ancient rest pavilions or sala samnak) (After A. Mollerup, 2004).

Notes on: 34. Villages

(1) The Chinese word **ta** (塔) can mean tower, or pagoda, or any tall structure; here, it could be a small Khmer temple or a stupa.

(2) The Chinese word **mai** (買) must be the transliteration of Khmer "mé" meaning chief or head, but **jie** (節) cannot be positively identified. Pelliot thought **mai jie** (買節) could be the transliteration of the Khmer word "mé srok" = chief of district. However, there is an archaic Khmer word "mé jee" meaning 'respectable elder' (Dictionnaire Cambodgien 1967). This word "mé jee" sounds very similar to **Zhou**'s **mai jie**.

(3) **Senmu** (森木) must be Zhou's transliteration of the Khmer word samnak = temporary stay. Researchers have identified stone monuments along Royal roads, such as the one from Angkor to Pimai (Mollerup 2004, Im Sokrithy 2005, Im Sokrithy & Surat Lertlum 2015). A stone inscription in Sanskrit at Preah Khan mentioned Vahnigṛha or 'houses with fire' (Coedès 1941) that Foucher (1903) called 'gites d'étapes' = 'rest houses'. Finot (1925) suggested the name Dharmasala since the building style mixes civic and religious character. Wooden sala samnak existed along national roads up to the 1950s , but were destroyed during the 1970s civil war. Some communities rebuilt them as shown in Fig. 34-02.

Fig. 34-02. A modern day "sala samnak" (rest-pavilion) in Kien Svay village along National Route No. 1 (Photo S. Uk, 2006).

35
COLLECTING GALL BLADDERS

In the past, gall bladders[1] were collected in the 8th lunar month because every year the king of Champa demanded a jar with thousands of human gall bladders. At night, men were placed at various spots in the cities or villages where people would pass. When encountering a passerby, they would put a sack on their [victim's] head, restrain him with a rope, then use a small knife to take the gall bladder out from the lower right side. When the number was enough, the jar was presented to the king of Champa. But they do not take the gall bladders of Chinese because one year, they mixed one Chinese gall bladder with those of the locals and the whole jar was spoiled and became useless. Recently, gall bladder collecting has been abolished. Those ex-gall bladder collecting officials and their subordinates were made to live inside the city near the north gate.

Notes on: 35. Collecting Gall Bladders

(1) There is a Khmer name for a gall bladder collector, "prâmāt prâmâng". Gall bladder collecting had become a legend that country people used to frighten mischievous toddlers –"Stop crying, or the prâmātt prâmâng will come to get you", the saying goes. There is the belief that drinking the enemy's bile would cure illnesses and make a man strong and invincible in battle. Unfortunately, this gruesome belief and the practice of eating the liver and drinking the bile of the enemy in battle still existed among some soldiers during the two Indochina wars in the 20th century [eating the enemy's liver kills his soul (Thach Toan 2009)]. In China, the word **dan** (膽) (gall bladder) implies bravery.

36
AN EXTRAORDINARY STORY

Inside the east gate, there was a barbarian who had sex with his younger sister. Then their skin and flesh were stuck together [and] could not be separated. After three days without eating, they died. One countryman from my home town area, Mr. **Xue** who has lived in this country for 35 years said that he had witnessed this phenomenon twice. The reason is the power of the holy Buddha spirit. That is why it is so.

37
BATHING

This place is dreadfully hot; one would not be able to endure it without bathing many times each day. Even at night, one would bathe once or twice. Earlier, there were no bathrooms, wash bowls or buckets, but each house had to have a pool, or otherwise two or three houses share a pool.

Both men and women get into the pool together naked. When the parents or elderly people are already in the pool then the children, servants, or young people dare not get in. If the servants or young people are already in the pool, the elderly would also avoid it. People of the same age group are uninhibited with each other. They use only their left hand to cover their private parts and go into the water. Sometimes every three or four, or every five or six days, city women in groups of three to five would go to bathe in the river outside the city. They arrive at the river bank, take off the cloths that wrap their bodies, go into the water, and meet other groups in the river. Sometimes there can be thousands of people. Even women from the noble families do the same and do not consider it shameful. They can all be seen from head to heel.

In the big river outside the city, there is not one day without this scene. The Chinese with free time, like to go and watch for pleasure. I have heard that some of them get into the water and 'steal some desire and hope'. This water is always as warm as soup; not until the fifth watch does it get slightly cooler. In the morning after the sun rises, it warms up again.

Fig. 37-01. Chidren bathing in a hot day in a pond inside the wall of Prasat Preah Khan in Angkor (Photo S. Uk, 2011).

38
IMMIGRATION

The Chinese sailors find it favorable that in this country clothing is not necessary. Also rice is easy to find and women easy to obtain. Housing is easy to maintain; it is easy to make do with few utensils and tools, and trade is easy to run. Therefore, most of them deserted to settle here (Fig. 38-01).

Fig. 38-01. Chinese residents in a cooking session (Bayon bas-relief) (Photo S. Uk, 2006).

39
THE ARMY

Riding soldiers are also bare-bodied and barefooted. They hold a spear in their right hands and shields in their left. They do not have bows and arrows, ballista or body armour[1]. I have heard that in the war with the Siamese, civilians were drafted to fight mostly without wise strategies or planned tactics.

Fig. 39-01. Soldiers with bows and arrows, and crossbows (Bayon bas-relief) (Photo S. Uk, 2006).

Notes on 39: The Army

(1) It is strange that **Zhou Daguan** mentioned that soldiers had neither bows and arrows nor body armour, whereas sculptures on the gallery walls of the Bayon and Angkor Wat have many scenes of parading troops with bows & arrows, crossbows and ballistae (Figs. 39-01 & 39-02). **Zhou** may have been mistaken (Murray 2002). Furthermore, those temples may have been strictly for the king's use in royal ceremonies and pious acts, and may not be opened freely to the public not least to a foreigner.

Fig. 39-02. Ballistae on an elephant's back and on a cart in a military parade (Bayon bas-relief) (Photo S. Uk, 1999).

40

THE KING'S MOVEMENTS OUT AND INTO THE PALACE

Translators' Note: To keep the translation faithful to Zhou's words, the chapter title is opposite to the normal English expression "The king's Movement In and Out of the Palace". Chinese use the expression **chu ru** (**chu** (出) = "go out ", and **ru** (入) = "enter").

I have heard of the previous king[1] that the tracks of his chariot wheels never left the palace residence for fear of incidents. The new king is the son-in-law of the previous king. His original profession was being in charge of the soldiers. His father-in-law was very fond of his daughter, and the daughter secretly stole the golden sword to give to her husband. This is the reason that the king's own son could not succeed him to the throne and thus he planned a military coup. The new king discovered the plot, caught him, cut off his toes, and put him in a dark chamber.

This new king has a piece of 'holy iron'[2] embedded in his body, so that he cannot be harmed by a knife or arrow. Because of this, he dares go out of his palace. During my stay of over[3] a year, I have seen this king go out four or five times. Every time he goes out, there are horse-mounted troops in front, and flag carriers, drummers and musicians at the rear. There are three to five hundred palace women wearing floral patterned dresses, with flowers inserted in their hair buns, and they carry huge candles and form their own group. The candles are lit even in bright daylight. Also there are some palace women carrying gold and silverware and scripted ornaments of a particular design. I do not know for what purpose these are. There are other palace women who carry spears and shields as 'inner' soldiers and form another contingent.

In the procession there are also goat carts and horse carts, all decorated in gold. All high officials and members of the royal family ride elephants at the front. From the distance one sees an overwhelming number of red parasols. Next are the king's wives and concubines riding on palanquins, carts, horses, or elephants, all with gold speckled parasols that number surely over a hundred at

Fig. 40-01. Stôb (containing permanent sacrificial fire) procession that always precedes the King's outing (Bayon's bas-relief, west wall) (Photo S. Uk, 2012).

Fig. 40-02. King's outing (South gallery of Angkor Wat) (Photo S. Uk, 2001).

least. After this, comes the king standing on the back of an elephant, holding the precious sword. The tusks of the elephants are sheathed in gold. All around the king, there are more than twenty white parasols with gold speckles. The handles of these parasols are all made of gold. There are numerous elephants surrounding the king. Also there are riding soldiers for his protection.

For short outings, the king only uses a golden palanquin carried by the palace women. Normally during the king's trips in and out of the palace, he must welcome[4] a small golden **ta**[5] and a golden Buddha statue that are carried in front [of him]. All spectators must kneel and bow their heads to the ground, which is called '**sanba**'[6], otherwise they would be arrested by the officers in charge and would not be released lightly.

The king holds audiences[7] twice daily, but does not follow definite written procedures. If the officials and citizens wish to see the king, they all sit on the ground to form a queue and wait. After a while, light music comes from inside, and outside a conch shell is blown to welcome the king. I have heard that only a golden cart is used when he comes from a bit further away. After a short while two palace women can be seen rolling up the blind with their slender delicate hands, and the king holding the sword, standing inside the golden window. The ministers, officials and others all put their hands together and kowtow. Not until the sound of the conch stops, are they allowed to raise their heads. The king then sits down. The sitting place has a lion skin that is the royal hereditary treasure. After all matters are finished, the king turns around and the two palace women let down the blind again. Everyone rises. From this, one can see that even in a barbarian country, one does not fail to know who is the king.

Notes on: 40. The King's Movements Out and Into the Palace

(1) King Jayavarman VIII: He was apparently very old in 1295 (Giteau 1999). He was a fanatical follower of Śivaism and destroyed many Buddhist symbols in many monuments built by his predecessor, the Buddhist King Jayavarman VII. During his reign, the country was divided by religious strife. He was forced to abdicate in 1295 (Giteau 1999) after his daughter stole the golden sword (symbol of the throne) and gave it to her husband who became King Indravarman III. He deprived Jayavarman VIII's son of the throne by arresting him, cutting off his toes, and putting him in jail.

(2) **Jin Ronghua: sheng tie** (聖鐵) = holy iron, made of bone; used as a talisman. Now talismans made of copper, lead, silver, or gold are still in use by believers.

(3) According to **Zhou**'s description in his Introduction, he stayed slightly less than one year in Angkor.

(4) The original text '**bi ying xiao jin ta jin fo zai qi qian**' (必迎小金塔金佛在其前) literally means 'must greet/welcome a small golden **ta** and a gold Buddha are in front'. The word **ying** (迎) literally means 'meet, greet, welcome, receive'. In this context the king welcomes the stupa (**ta** 塔) and the golden Buddha that are brought along and put in front of him during his outings. The same word **ying** appears in Chapter 13 when **Zhou** described the festival of 'Welcome Buddha Water'.

(5) Small golden **ta**: This word **ta** (塔) refers to the Khmer word "stôb" meaning 'miniature stupa'. What **Zhou Daguan** described as "stupa" could be the container for Permanent Sacrificial Fire (Kandvar Homa) that always accompanies the King in all his processions outside the palace (Vong Sotheara 2011) (Fig. 40-01).

(6) Transliteration of Khmer word "sâmpeah" = to kowtow.

(7) Example of a king's outing (Fig. 40-02).

APPENDICES

APPENDIX A

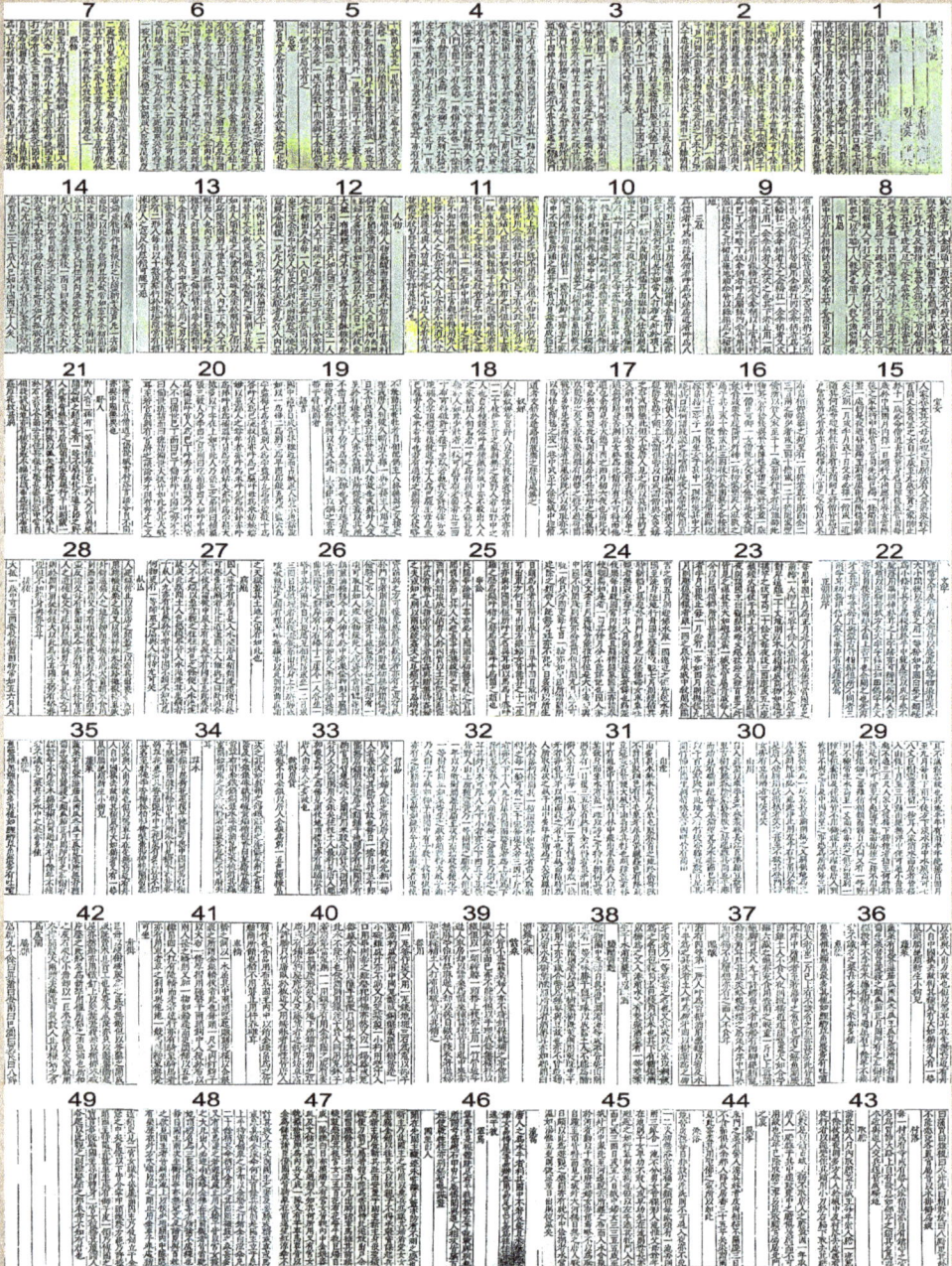

Appendix A. Copy of the block prints of the Wu Guan edition of Zhou Daguan's Record. The pages have been rearranged side by side to read from right to left and top to bottom

APPENDIX B

Order of the Khmer Luni-Solar Months

The months' Sanskrit names are put in brackets. The corresponding Khmer solar months (middle column) have the same number of days and cycle as in the Gregorian calendar (right hand column), i.e. the 1st month is Makara which corresponds to January, etc.

Current order of lunar months (Sanskrit name)	Current Khmer solar months	Gregorian months
01.Mégasir (Mārgaśīrṣa)	Vichikā- Dhnū	November-December
02. Bós (Pausa)	Dhnū- Makara	December - January
03. Miákh (Māgha)	Makara-Komphéak	January - February
04. Phalkún (Phālguna)	Kompéak-Mína	February - March
05. Chèt (Chaitra)	Mína - Mésā	March - April
06 Vîssàkh (Vaiśākha)	Mésā - Usáphea	April - May
07 Chés (Jyeṣṭha)	Usáphea - Míthunā	May - June
08 Asádh (Āṣāḍha)	Míthunā - Kakkadā	June - July
09 Sráp (Śrāvaṇa)	Kakkadā - Sihā	July - August
10. Photrobot (Bhādrapada)	Sihā - Kanhā	August - September
11. Āsoch (Āśvina)	Kanhā - Túlā	September - October
12. Kâdëk (Kārttika)	Túlā - Vichikā	October - November

N.B. Unique to modern Cambodia: the numerical order of the lunar months does not begin on the New Year. By following the ancient Hindu system, the Khmer New Year begins with the alignment of the constellation Chaitra, with the sun and the earth that occurs every year around the 12th and 14th of April. Thus, the name of the Khmer luni-solar year (as well as the Buddhist year) does not change until after April 13th or 14th, i.e., on the 5th lunar month or the 4th solar month.

Selected References

In Chinese:

1. 陳正祥 (**Chen Zhengxiang**). 1969. 真臘風土記的研究 (**Zhenla feng tu ji de yan jiu**). 香港: 地理研究中心 (**Xiang gang: Di li yan jiu zhong xin**).

2. 金榮華 (**Jin Ronghua**).1976. 真臘風土記校注 (**Zhenla feng tu ji jiao zhu**). 國民文庫1.(**Guo min wen ku 1**). 台灣, 台北 (**Taiwan, Taibei**):正中書局 (**Zheng zhong shu ju**).

3. 李晨阳 等 (**Li Chen-yang**, et al.). 2005. 柬埔寨 (Cambodia).列国志 (Guide to the World States). 北京 (**Beijing**): 社会科学文献出版社 (**she hui ke xue wen xian chu ban she**).

4. 夏鼐 (**Xia Nai**). 2000. 真臘風土記校注 (**Zhenla feng tu ji jiao zhu**). 中外交通史籍叢刊4 (**Zhong wai jiao tong shi ji cong kan, 4**).北京 (**Beijing**): 中華書局 (**zhong hua shu ju**).

5. 景印文淵閣四庫全書 第五九四冊 (**Yingyin Wenyuange，Si ku quan shu – vol. 594**). 1983. 臺灣(**Taiwan**): 商務印書館 (**shang wu yin shu guan**).

6. 新華漢語詞典 (**Xinhua Hanyu Cidian**). 2007. 北京(**Beijing**): 商務印書館 (**shang wu yin shu guan**).

7. 漢英詞典 (**Hanying Cidian**), A Chinese-English Dictionary. 1979. 北京 (**Beijing**): 商務印書館 (**shang wu yin shu guan**).

8. 新時代英漢大詞典 (New Age English-Chinese Dictionary). 2004. 北京 (**Beijing**): 商務印書館 (**shang wu yin shu guan**).

In Roman Alphabets:

Abel-Rémusat, Jean Pierre (1819) *Description du Royaume de Cambodge* (*Traduite du Chinois*). Kessinger Legacy Reprint : Kessinger Publishing, LLC.

Aczel, A. D. (2015) *Finding Zero. A Mathematician's Odyssey to Uncover the Origins of Numbers*. New York: Palgrave Macmillan Trade.

Aschmoneit, Walter (2006) *Zhou Daguan. Aufzeichnungen über die Gebräuche Kambodschas*. Berlin: Studiengemeinschaft Kambodschanische Kultur e.V.

Briggs, Lawrence Palmer (1951) *The Ancient Khmer Empire*. Philadephia: Transaction of the American Philosophical Society, vol. 41 (Part 1).

Chandler, D. P. (1979) *Folk memories of the decline of Angkor in nineteenth-century Cambodia: The legend of the Leper King.* Journal of the Siam Society 67: 54 – 62.

Chandler, D. P. (2000) *A History of Cambodia.* 3rd ed. Oxfod: Westview Press.

Chay Son (2008) *Personal communication.*

Coedès, George (1941) *La stèle de Prāh Khān d'Ankor,* Bulletin de l'Ecole Française d'Extrême Orient 41: 255-302"

Coedès, George (1961) *Angkor: An Introduction.* Oxford: Oxford University Press.

Coedès, George (1989) *Articles sur le Pays Khmer.* Paris: Ecole Française d'Extrême Orient.

Dagens, Bruno (2005) *Les Khmers.* Guide Belles Lettres des Civilisations. Paris: Société d'édition Les Belles Lettres.

Davidson, Peter (2009) *Birds of Vietnam, Cambodia and Laos.* London: New Holland Publishers.

Dema (2006) *Personal communication.* Ulaan Baator: Mongolia Discovery Tours.

Dictionnaire Cambodgien. (in Khmer) (1967). Phnom Penh: Institut Bouddhique.

Dumarçay, Jacques (1973) *Le Bayon: Histoire Architecturale du Temple.* Mémoires Archeologiques III-2. Paris: Ecole Française d'Extrême Orient (ed Adrien-Maisonneuve).

Dy Phon, Pauline (2000) *Dictionary of Plants Used in Cambodia.* Phnom-Penh: Hor Thim "Imprimerie Olympic".

Eng Soth (1969) *The Khmer Royalty* History (in Khmer). Phnom-Penh: Great Khmer Personalities Records No. 67.

Evans, D., et al. (2013) *Uncovering archaeological landscapes at Angkor using lidar.* Proceedings Nat'l Academy of Sciences, vol. 110 (31): 12595 – 12600.

Finot, Louis (1925) *Dharmaçâlâs au Cambodge.* Bulletin de l'Ecole Française d'Extrême Orient 25: 417–422.

Finot, Louis and Victor Goloubew (1930) *Rapport sur une mission archeologique à Ceylon.* Bulletin de l'Ecole Française d'Extrême Orient 30: 627 - 643.

Foucher, A. (1903) *Les édicules des gîtes d'étapes.* Journal Asiatique, I, 10ème Série: 179-180.

Freeman, M. and Jacques, C. (2006) *Ancient Angkor.* Bangkok: River Book Ltd.

Gangstad, E.O., Seaman, D.E., and Nelson, M.L. (1972) *Potential growth of aquatic plants of the lower Mekong River basin Laos-Thailand.* Journal of Aquatic Plant Management 10: 4-9.

Garnier, Francis (1985) *Voyage d'Exploration en Indo-Chine Effectué Par Une Commission Française.* Paris: Librairie Hachette et Cie.

Giteau, Madeleine (1974) *Histoire d'Angkor.* Paris: Presses Universitaires de France (ed Que sais-je?).

Giteau, Madeleine (1999) *Histoire d'Angkor.* Paris: Kailash.

Glaize, Maurice (2003) *Les Monuments du Groupe d'Angkor*. Paris: Jean Maisonneuve.

Goloubew, Victor (1935) *Sylvain Levy et l'Indochine*. Bulletin de l'Ecole Française d'Extrême Orient 35: 550-574.

Groslier, Bernard Philippe (1973) *Inscriptions du Bayon*. Mémoires Archeologiques III-2. Paris: Ecole Française d'Extrême Orient (ed Adrien-Maisonneuve).

Harris, Peter (2007) *A Record of Cambodia*: The Land and Its People. Chiang Mai: Silkworm Book.

Higham, Charles (1989) *The Archeology of Mainland Southeast Asia*. New York: Cambridge University Press.

Higham, Charles (2001) *The Civilization of Angkor*. London: Phoenix.

Hoc Cheng Siny (2001) Le touk khmer. Techniques & Culture, 35-36: 509-521.

Im Sokrithy (2005) *Angkorian Road Network and its Intertwined Structure* (In Khmer). Apsara Authority, Cambodia.

Im Sokrithy and Surat Lertlum (2015) *The Living Angkor Road Project: Connectivity within Ancient Mainland Southeast Asia*. Center for Southeast Asian Studies, Kyoto University Newsletter, No. 71, March 2015

Jacques, Claude (1990) *Angkor*. Paris: Bordas S.A.

Johnson, Denis (1992) *Palm utilization and management in Asia: Examples for the neotropics*. Bulletin de l'Institut Français d'Etudes Andines 21 (2): 727-740.

Kham, Lavit (2004) *Medicinal Plants of Cambodia*. Golden Square, Australia: Bendigo Scientific Press.

Ly Thiam Teng (1973) *Zhou Daguan's Record: On the Customs of Zhenla* (in Khmer). Phnom-Penh: Moha Leap.

Malleret, Louis (1963) *L'archéologie du delta du Mekong, vol.43, no.4*. Paris: Ecole Française d'Extrême Orient.

Mannika, E. (1996) *Angkor Wat: Time, Space, and Kingship*. Honolulu: University of Hawai'i Press.

Marchal, Henri (1928) *Guide Archeologique aux Temples d'Angkor*. Paris: G. van Oest.

Marchal, Henri (1955) *Les Temples d'Angkor*. Paris: Albert Guillot.

Maspéro, Georges (1928) *Le Royaume de Champa*. Paris: G. van Oest.

Mollerup, Asger (2004) *The Dharmasala Route from Angkor to Phimai*, www.sundial. thai-isan-lao.com/dharmasalaroute.html

Murray, S. O. (2002) *Angkor Life*. Bangkok: Floating Lotus Communications Co.

Narang, Nouth and Groslier, Bernard Philippe (2003) *La Cité Hydraulique Angkorienne, Fondement de la Civilisation Khmère* (in Khmer). Phnom-Penh: Resource and Research Center on Khmer Civilization.

Narang, Nouth (2011) *Personal communication*.

Oldroyd, B. P. and Wongsiri, S. (2006) *Asian Honey Bees*. Cambridge: Harvard University Press.

Pelliot, Paul (1997) *Mémoires sur les Coutumes du Cambodge de Tcheou Ta-Kuan*. Paris: Adrien Maisonneuve. [Reprinting of the original 1951 edition].

Smithies, Michael (2001) *The Customs of Cambodia by Zhou Daguan* (Chou Ta-Kuan). Bangkok: The Siam Society.

Porée, Guy and Maspéro, Eveline (1938) *Moeurs et Coutumes des Khmèrs*. Paris: Payot.

Porée-Maspéro, Eveline (195?) *Cérémonies des Douze Mois*. Commission des Moeurs et Coutumes du Cambodge. Phnom-Penh: Albert Portail.

Pou Saveros (2004) *Dictionnaire Vieux Khmer-Français-Anglais*. Paris: L'Harmattan.

Sahai, Sachchidanand (2007) *The Bayon of Angkor Thom*. Bangkok: White Lotus.

Schweyer, Anne-Valérie (2004) *Les relations entre le pays khmer et le pays cham: Les frères ennemis*. Notre Histoire 217: 26-29.

Suon Pheav (1999) *Province of Kampong Chhnang*. Geography of Cambodia (in Khmer). Phnom-Penh.

Tia Then (2005) *The Affairs of Kampuchea Krom (Former Cochinchina)* (in Khmer). Phnom Penh: Indratevi Publishing.

Thach Toan (2009) *Histoire des Khmers: L'Odyssée du Peuple Cambodgien*. Paris: L'Harmattan.

Tum, Phylypo (2008) *Khmer New Year*. WWW.Cam-CC.org. Long Beach: Cambodian Coordinating Council.

Vong Sotheara (2003) *Stone Inscriptions of Cambodia before Angkor Period, vol.1*. Campbell: Buddhi Khmer Center.

Vong Sotheara (2011) *Personal communication*.

Walker Vadillo, V. Nautical (2015) Angkor: An iconological study of Khmer vessels in Angkorian bas-relefs. *In: Maritime Contact of the Past – Deciphering Connections Amongst Communities*. Sila Tripati, ed. New Delhi, Delta Book Word.

Yam, Chhann (2009) *Personal communication*

Zhang Chunguang. (2007) *China Animal Information System. Catalogue of Life*. **Beijing**: The Biodiversity Committee of Chinese Academy of Sciences.

INDEX

ជីវតាគ្មាន់
កំណត់ហេតុអំពី
ទឹកដី និង ប្រពៃណីប្រទេសកម្ពុជា

周达观撰
真腊风土记

បកប្រែសម្រួលពីឯកសារដើមភាសាចិន និងធ្វើអត្ថាធិប្បាយ
ដោយ អ៊ិក សុឡួង និង អ៊ិក ប៉ាវបេលិង

– Zhou Daguan Ed. 2 in Khmer –
Available at Peace Book Center in Phnom Penh.